THE
EVERYTHING

PREGNANCY
ORGANIZER

The Everything® Pregnancy Series:

The Everything® Pregnancy Book
The Everything® Get Ready for Baby Book
The Everything® Baby Names Book
The Everything® Get Ready for Baby Mini Book
The Everything® Pregnancy Organizer

THE
EVERYTHING
PREGNANCY
ORGANIZER

Monthly checklists, calendars, schedules, and more

Marguerite Smolen

Adams Media Corporation
Holbrook, Massachusetts

An Everything® Series Book
Everything® is a registered trademark of Adams Media Corporation.

Published by
Adams Media Corporation
260 Center Street, Holbrook, MA 02343
adamsmedia.com

ISBN: 1-58062-336-0

Printed in Korea.

J I H G F E D C B

Cataloging-in-publication information available
from the publisher upon request.

This publication is designed to provide accurate and authoritative information with regard to the subject matter covered. It is sold with the understanding that the publisher is not engaged in rendering professional medical advice. If assistance is required, the services of a competent professional person should be sought.

Illustrations by Barry Littmann

This book is available at quantity discounts for bulk purchases. For information, call 1-800-872-5627.

Visit our Web site at http://www.adamsmedia.com

Contents

PART ONE
THE FIRST TRIMESTER

MONTH ONE 1

Part Two
The Second Trimester

Part Three
The Third Trimester

APPENDIX A

APPENDIX B

APPENDIX C

Introduction

Congratulations! You're pregnant! Once the shock begins to wear off, you're probably going to have a lot of questions about the whole process—not to mention a lot to do! But don't worry, this book is designed to help you make the next nine months as stress-free as possible.

In order to get through labor and delivery, we've broken down the overwhelming experience into small, simple steps. We've included worksheets, planning calendars, charts, and checklists so you can keep all the essential information in one easy-to-use handbook. And its convenient size means you can take it with you to the many appointments you will have over the next few months. Feeling nervous? Don't. Just keep this book handy and you'll have everything covered.

Begin the calendar portion with the first day of your last period, even if it didn't fall on the first day of the month. This is an important date to remember; your doctor will require it to determine your due date. You'll also need the date for your ultrasound appointment, as well as other important tests.

Next, count out forty weeks—or 280 days—from the first day of your last period. This will be your "due date." In most pregnancies it is almost impossible to determine the exact moment of conception, and this is the best way doctors can approximate when you will deliver. Mark this date on the calendar; it should fall on the very last page.

In between, fill out the months and days. While the calendar will look different than a standard calendar, to you it will serve a much more important function. And toward the end of your pregnancy, you'll surely be counting the days until the baby arrives.

Have fun with the calendar, and use it for every aspect of your pregnancy. It can serve as an accessible reminder to know exactly what week you are in, and to keep track of doctor's appointments, scheduled tests, and when to expect their results. Use it as a diary or journal, where you can jot down your thoughts and feelings on particular days that are important to you; the day you first felt the baby kick, the day you stopped feeling queasy, the day your regular clothes stopped fitting, your first shopping trip to the maternity store, the day you somehow "knew" just what the sex of the baby would be. Or anything else that you will want to remember or later share with your new child.

This calendar can be used as a way to keep track of your weight gain. You can even keep a record of what you've been eating to make sure that you are getting a balanced diet and enough calories as your pregnancy progresses.

Part One

The First Trimester

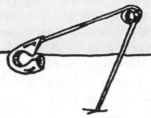

Month One

Looking for bathrooms everywhere,
Old familiar taste buds gone haywire,
Shaky? Scared? Ecstatic? . . . Happy!

TO DO THIS MONTH

- ❏ *Buy a pregnancy test kit.*
- ❏ *Write down your symptoms.*
- ❏ *Find a doctor.*
- ❏ *Learn about what's happening inside your body.*
- ❏ *Figure out your due date*
- ❏ *Get your questions answered.*

The first month is filled with excitement as you realize that you are going to experience the incredible process of growing a baby and giving birth to it. You may feel scared, nervous, happy, sick, ecstatic, energetic, or any of the above. In addition to all of the emotional excitement, you'll need to deal with the lifestyle habits that you've accumulated up till now. The first month should be devoted to establishing positive habits that will bring you and your baby through this challenging physical and emotional experience healthfully. So,

- Take time now to learn all you can about the stages of pregnancy and how to take care of yourself.
- Schedule time each week to read about pregnancy, especially about good health and nutrition.
- Start cutting back on unnecessary time commitments.
- Begin simplifying your lifestyle so that you can enjoy the process of being pregnant and have a low-stress pregnancy in the months ahead.

This Month's Priorities

Congratulations are in order! At last—you've dreamed of becoming pregnant, and now, you're pretty sure you are. To confirm the good news, you'll want to:

- ❏ Buy a pregnancy test kit, and test yourself at home.
- ❏ Write down your symptoms.
- ❏ Find a doctor.
- ❏ Make an appointment to get checked out.

Confirming Your Pregnancy

Approximately two weeks after conception or just one day after you miss your period, an obstetrician, nurse-midwife, or clinic practitioner can confirm your pregnancy by testing a sample of your urine and examining you internally. What a pregnancy test, or *immunoassay*, is actually measuring the circulating hormone *human chorionic gonadotropin*, (HCG), produced by pregnancy tissues and present in both your blood and your urine after conception. However, it is very difficult to detect any changes in a uterus one day after a skipped period. Only when implantation has occurred (this happens at days 6 through 10) are these tell-tale hormones being excreted. So it isn't until ten to fourteen days that you can begin to detect a pregnancy.

Home pregnancy kits, available in most pharmacies, may be the fastest route to answer this major life question: Are you pregnant? Follow the package directions carefully. Kits rely on a chemical. When combined with your urine in a little test tube, this chemical will change colors in the presence of HCG.

Finding the Right Medical Help

Finding the right medical professional(s) to help guide you through this very important year of your life is absolutely essential. If you don't already have a doctor you trust and with whom you feel comfortable and confident, start investigating now. If your gynecologist also practices obstetrics, your search might be over, especially if you are in a high-risk category. A specialist could be important in an emergency.

- Check your health insurance coverage to see if the plan has a list of approved obstetrical practices.
- Your family practitioner can help or may even be able to monitor your pregnancy and deliver your baby.
- Certified nurse-midwives are an option for some women.

Finding Referrals
- Call your county medical society and ask for the names of three obstetricians practicing in your geographical area.

Ask friends, coworkers, neighbors, and other doctors for rec-ommendations, as well as your health care provider. Collect beautiful birth stories so you can create your own dream come true by using ideas that helped make everything go so beautifully for other expectant couples.

- Call the nearest hospital or your favorite major medical center and describe your situation. Be specific. For instance, if you think you'd like to have a woman doctor, and preferably someone with a midwife on staff, say so. If you've read about the benefits of some aspect of labor and delivery—a birthing room, for instance—ask about it right away. By the way, a hospital's approach to childbirth may even determine the doctor or practice you choose. If you like the hospital, ask about practitioners who have medical privileges established there.
- The American College of Obstetricians and Gynecologists (ACOG) and the American College of Nurse-Midwives (ACONM) also provide lists of resources. (See Appendix, "Important Names and Addresses.")
- *The Directory of Medical Specialists* features not only the doctor's name and specialty, but also where he or she went to school, the affiliated hospital, address, phone number, and even age and birthplace. Check it out at your local library.

Important Note: You can check the credentials of any physician in a specialty by telephoning the American Board of Medical Specialists' hotline: 1-800-776-2378. Obstetricians and gynecologists are specialists who have received extra training and have passed certifying examinations in their area of expertise.

The First Appointment

When you've narrowed down your choices for a team of profession-als to steer your pregnancy, telephone the office and explain to the nurse or receptionist that you are pregnant and have questions to ask about the practice. Keep in mind that many obstetric, childbirth,

Who Will Deliver the Baby?

Name: _____

Address: _____

_____

_____

Phone Number: _____

Receptionist's Name: _____

Nurses Name(s): _____

_____

_____

Affiliated Hospital: _____

_____

Payments Due: _____

_____

Lab Address and Phone Number: _____

_____

_____

Notes: _____

_____

_____

_____

_____

_____

_____

_____

Once you are under the care of a particular physician or group practice, you'll have lots of question-and-answer sessions on a regular basis, but a little preliminary research will go a long way toward establishing a wonderful rapport later. You just don't want to be shocked later when you discover something disturbing about your doctor's policy. You are much better off asking upfront. Don't worry about appearing to be too inquisitive. Ask away. Among the questions you might want to ask are:

1. *How much will it cost?* Check your health insurance policy to find out how pregnancy is handled. Ask the doctor how much your pregnancy will cost and exactly what the fee includes.

   _____

   _____

2. *Can my husband or friend stay with me during labor and delivery?* This sounds like a concern from the dark ages, but you may want to hear the official policy on visitors at these crucial times.

   _____

   _____

3. *Who will deliver my baby?* If the doctor is a sole practitioner, ask about backup care. You'll want to know the practitioner he or she uses to fill in on vacations, for instance. However, if you are a patient in a group of childbirth professionals, you may want to talk about your need to get to know all the specialists during the nine months so you aren't greeted by a stranger when you go into labor and suddenly get the doctor on call for that particular night or day.

   _____

   _____

4. *Will I be able to move around during labor?* Some experts believe that lying flat on your back during your entire labor can actually slow the process. Perhaps you need to know how the doctor feels about laboring women doing laps through the hospital corridor. (For more about hospitals, birthing centers, and home births, see pages 222–227.)

   _____

   _____

5. *What is your policy on amniocentesis, pain medication, routine fetal monitoring, or drugs to induce labor?*

   _____

   _____

6. *Will I stay in my room to deliver the baby or be moved to a special delivery suite?*

   _____

   _____

7. *How do you feel about episiotomies?* An episiotomy is a cut sometimes made between the vagina and the anus near the very end of labor to help the baby's head pass through. (See Month Nine for more about episiotomies.)

   _____

   _____

8. *How long will I stay in the hospital after the birth?* Some insurance companies also have policies on this question of recuperation time in the hospital. Find out what your plan specifies, and ask the doctor if he or she ever intervenes to extend the stay. Ask what the hospital visiting hours are.

   _____

   _____

Questions to Ask

9. *Is there a special neonatal unit?* If not, where will any baby who needs extra help be transferred? Though you don't want to anticipate trouble, knowing exactly how the doctor and hospital handle emergencies is important.

   _____

   _____

10. *What is your approach to weight gain during pregnancy?* Some physicians are known for watching their patients closely and actually trying to manage weight gain. Others take a more laid-back approach, knowing that, in many cases, weight is not easily controlled or predictable during pregnancy.

    _____

    _____

11. *What can I expect from regular prenatal office visits?* In fact, how often will you find yourself in the office? Will checkups differ from your gynecological examinations?

    _____

    _____

    Other

    _____

    _____

    _____

    _____

    _____

    _____

    _____

    _____

and midwifery practices are very busy during patient visiting hours. Don't push for immediate details right there on that first phone call. Ask about a time of day when exploratory calls like yours might be easier to handle. However, listen closely to the tone of voice you hear on your initial telephone connection. Even very busy professionals can demonstrate their potential for kindness. Don't put up with rudeness. You are about to hire someone to help you through one of the most important undertakings of your life.

The Physical Exam

The first visit may be one of the longest because it will include a thorough physical exam, complete with blood tests, weight and height checks, and health history. Even if the nurse or receptionist doesn't indicate how long it will take, to be safe, set aside extra time, especially if you are taking off from work.

Your Medical History

You will want to ask a lot of questions, and, as well, you'll have to answer a lot in this first session. Some of the questions you can expect the doctor to raise are:

- *What is your blood type?* The doctor will check for the presence of what is known as the rhesus, or Rh factor that can complicate your pregnancy.
- *Is your cervix is closed tightly?* An internal exam will assure the doctor it is.
- *Do you have any disease?* The doctor will want to know about sexually transmitted diseases as well as other conditions such as sickle cell anemia. If you've had German measles and can remember when, this also will go on your chart because, though it is a common childhood disease, it can be a problem in pregnancy.

The Checkup

At each visit, you'll go through the same basic steps. Here they are:

⚕ *You'll give a urine sample.*

At each visit, you will be asked to urinate into a little cup, in private. After showing you to the examination room, asking you to take off your clothes and slip into the gown, the nurse or assistant will routinely hand you a little plastic cup and direct you to the nearest bathroom. Most women have no problem going to the bathroom frequently during pregnancy. Even a small sample is just fine. What your practitioner is looking for are traces of sugar that might indicate that you are developing diabetes. He or she also checks for signs of protein, which is a warning that your kidneys aren't working properly. Late in pregnancy, if the presence of protein is detected, it signals a serious condition called *preeclampsia*, in which your blood pressure rises and you risk suffering convulsions.

⚕ *Someone will weigh you.*

Get ready to gain. Pregnancy weight gain is not always as easily or steadily controlled as expectant mothers or doctors would prefer. The charts say that you should aim for a total gain of twenty-five to thirty pounds evenly added month by month in small increments. However, some women have months of wild growth and others where those numbers on the scale stay pretty steady. Somewhere in my second trimester after fitting the pregnancy textbook gains perfectly, I suddenly went up nearly seven pounds overnight. (Well, if not exactly overnight, I did gain almost instantaneously.)

⚕ *Your legs, ankles, and hands will be observed to check for swelling.*

The doctor or midwife will want to make sure that you aren't retaining fluids, so she or he will check your legs, ankles, or hands.

♂ *You'll listen to the baby's heartbeat.*
Not at the first visit, but at all subsequent ones, an electronic device called a fetoscope or a sensitive ultrasound instrument called a Doppler device, will soon let you and your doctor listen to the baby's heartbeat. Those first sounds of your unborn baby's heartbeat may appear near Week 10 but more certainly about Week 12. They are actually the first *real* proof that you are pregnant. Don't miss any opportunity to lend your own ear to the event. Later, after Week 18 to 20, a standard stethoscope will pick up the beat.

♂ *Your abdomen will be poked, prodded, and measured.*
To check the position of the womb at each stage, you may look forward to this step at every appointment.

♂ *You'll be given an internal (pelvic) examination.*
There aren't very many women (if any) who relish the idea of internal or pelvic examinations. The doctor or midwife is checking for signs to confirm the fact that you are really pregnant. Changes that a skilled childbirth practitioner looks for include your enlarging uterus, which begins to change shape from pear-like to globular; soft spots on the uterus where the embryo has implanted; and signs of throbbing blood vessels, which your practitioner may feel by putting his or her fingers across the vagina.

Like the urine or blood tests, there are objective pieces of evidence that are certainly important:

♂ *Goodell's sign.* Your vagina and cervix start to retain fluid and actually become softer when you are pregnant. Ordinarily, your cervix is hard, and, as one expert explained, it might even feel like the tip of your nose. After about six weeks of pregnancy, it becomes as soft as your lips. In women who have been pregnant before, this softening may begin even sooner than six weeks.

♂ *Hegar's sign.* The doctor or midwife inserts two fingers into your vagina in order to touch the uterus. If you are six weeks' pregnant, your uterus will be softer than normal.

♂ *Chadwick's sign.* The color of your vagina, vulva, and cervix will turn bluish or even violet after two months of pregnancy because of the increased blood congestion and dilation of veins.

If your pregnancy proceeds along without complications, you'll probably have appointments once a month at least for the first seven months of pregnancy. After that, you may be going more often, especially in the last month. Additionally, your doctor may enhance this basic exam with more tools of the trade, and you'll learn about them in the months ahead.

How Your Baby Grows

Your Baby's Beginnings

Around the fourteenth day after your last period, your body released a healthy egg. One of your mate's 400 million sperm passed into your vagina, through the soft mucus being secreted by your cervix, and entered the egg, fertilizing it. The sperm lost its tail, and its head began to swell. A single cell formed. From this tiny cell, your baby is growing.

Week One

Only a few hours after penetration, the fertilized egg, sometimes called a *zygote*, travels down the fallopian tube toward its destination in the uterus, or womb. It floats down your fallopian tube surrounded by nutrient cells. It will take six days to reach the uterus. As it travels, the first cell is dividing, dividing, and dividing again. The little fertilized ovum gradually becomes more complicated. From two cells, there are four. From four cells, there are soon eight, and so on. By the end of this first week, a nearly invisible, fertilized ovum may boast anywhere from more than one hundred cells all closely knit into a little ball and ready to move into your uterus. Experts sometimes refer to the fertilized ovum at this stage as a *morula*, which means mulberry in Latin. Inside your womb, the morula finds important nutrients—sugars, salts, and critical elements—for growth. Still floating, it will grow quickly and become more sophisticated as the cells start specializing and taking on different tasks. Some link up to create kidneys. Others complete a small heart to pump blood. Timing is precise, and the genetic blueprint, with 46 chromosomes from you and 46 chromosomes from your mate, lays a course for your unborn baby.

Weeks Two and Three

Once the zygote reaches the uterus, it takes eight to ten days for implantation. *Implantation* is the point at which the fertilized egg attaches itself to the soft, spongy, welcoming lining of your uterus. Little "fingers," or rooting *villi*, from the edges of the fertilized egg, reach out to touch you, often on the upper, back wall of the womb. Not only will this ovum develop into your baby, but a few of its rapidly dividing cells will become the placenta that nourishes your baby and the umbilical cord, too, which connects the two of you. You may also hear this fluid-filled cluster of cells, which looks something like a blister, referred to as a *blastocyst* now.

Noted physician Virginia Apgar describes what happens now: "The hollow cluster of new cells burrows its way into the lining of the uterus, pushing aside some of the maternal cells and destroying others, tapping into the maternal blood vessels and using maternal blood and cell bits for nourishment." One of the more amazing aspects of this process is that your own body doesn't reject such an invasion, see it as foreign, or try to destroy the little blastocyst, now perhaps the size of the head of a pin. Although your unborn baby's tissues may be very different from yours, your body's immune system doesn't treat them differently. Your biochemistry appears to undergo a dramatic attitude adjustment, accepting the "new kid on the block" peacefully.

Week Four Jan 26 - Feb 1

By now, the product of your conception has earned a new title, that of *embryo*. Can you imagine that your own little embryo has a tiny beating heart, which looks like a large bulge at the chest front? A rudimentary brain and spinal cord also are present, as are shallow pits on the sides of the head, which show where eyes and ears will later grow. In size, the embryo is anywhere from $^1/_4$-inch to $1^1/_{10}$-inches long.

By the end of the first four weeks of growth, some of the rapidly dividing cells inside this little "blister" form the placenta, growing more inroads into your uterine cavity and paving the way for its expanding job of nourishing the unborn baby. Inside, the embryo is lengthening and becoming encapsulated in what appears to be a water-tight balloon sac, called the *amnion*. Fluids from your own body fill the sac and cushion your baby from all the bumps, lumps, and movement in your busy life. Known as the amniotic fluid, this watery substance keeps a consistent temperature and provides a weightless environment that allows the developing baby to exercise and move around.

Another little sac appears next to the embryo. Called the *yolk sac*, this teeny cluster of cells always floats nearby, consists of tiny blood vessels, and provides the blood for the embryo, which is still too immature to do so for itself.

Other kinds of growth and activity are also taking place during the end of this first month. For example, a third, bubblelike shelter must house the embryo, the amnion, and the yolk sac. On one side of the chorion are numerous little villi that grow into your uterus and form intricate webbings of blood vessels, multiplying, crisscrossing, and interlocking constantly to feed the placenta and give the embryo everything it could possibly need, including the umbilical cord. Quietly, the frenzy of this one-month production builds. Cells work frantically. You've got a baby in the making.

At the End of the First Month

Take an imaginary look at your embryo near the very end of this fourth week, and you might be amazed at how very specialized the existing three layers of growing cells have become. From the outer layers will come your baby's nervous system as well as the skin, hair, oil, and sweat glands. Meanwhile, in the middle will form the muscles, bones, kidneys, blood vessels, connective tissues, and even genital glands. Inside, the deepest layer of cells will eventually become important systems such as the digestive, the lungs, and the urinary tract. Early signs of a mouth, face, and throat are in place. Speeding at an incredibly fast pace, the unborn baby's heart, a U-shaped tube that can be seen beneath the opening for the mouth, contracts, perhaps hesitantly at first, but regularly by the end of the fourth week.

What You Can Expect to Experience

Emotional Changes

Once you're pregnant, you may find yourself feeling moody, perhaps even racing from tears to euphoria. Rest assured, there is nothing wrong with you. You are just beginning an intense, life-altering experience, and it's only normal to be fearful, dreamy, ambivalent, anxious, moody, confused, and ecstatically happy. Your moodiness is actually referred to as "emotional liability," and it can affect all expectant mothers occasionally or all the time. Are you crying over silly problems? Are you having anxiety attacks? Are you feeling giddy with laughter at inappropriate occasions? Depressed? Confused? Fearful? Your hormones may be affecting your central nervous system, which can make you feel as if you were walking around in a daze. Think about premenstrual syndrome. Were you ever weepy, short-tempered, or irrational before you got your period? Your pregnancy hormones are having a similar effect. Try to think past your immediate emotions. Speak with your practitioner about your mood swings and ask for advice. Depression is never to be taken lightly, but the zany emotional swings pregnancy can produce are probably not serious signs of a clinical problem.

Fatigue

The level of hormones, estrogen, progesterone, and chorionic gonadotropin rise in your body during the first weeks of pregnancy, and your body needs time to adjust. You actually require more hours of sleep each night when you are pregnant. Remember when you were a teenager and could sleep all Saturday morning long if the people in your life would let you? Well, you need that kind of sleep now. Early pregnancy can demand just as much rest as adolescence. If you can't get to bed earlier at night or sleep late in the morning, plan some naptime. Even a few minutes rest during the day can reenergize you for hours. Meanwhile, if you are cranky and unable to think straight, don't try to forge ahead during the day. These are signs of exhaustion, so slow down. Your growing baby needs you to be relaxed and well rested.

Excessive Salivation

Known as *ptyalism*, excessive salivation is rare but usually shows up early in pregnancy and can last the entire nine months. Saliva can actually fill your mouth up to the point where you can't avoid spitting. The sour taste can be pretty awful as well. Some experts suggest using mouthwashes, rinsing with water regularly, sucking mints, candies, or lemon slices, brushing your teeth often, and even cutting down on the starches in your diet. Supposedly, starch aggravates the problem. Others suggest eating many small meals during the day and keeping an empty bowl next to your bed for spitting during the night. There are some medicines that can be used to control ptyalism. Consult your doctor.

Feeling Faint

Blood pressure is lower when you are pregnant, and you are more likely to feel faint. Don't jump up quickly after you've been sitting or lying down. In fact, turn your body to one side when you are climbing out of bed. Anticipate occasions when you know you will be forced to stand up for long stretches and be prepared to sit anywhere. When you feel dizzy, light-headed, or wobbly, sit down and put your head between your knees. This symptom of feeling faint usually passes in the second trimester, although you may experience it again at the end of your pregnancy.

Taking Care of Yourself

Menu Planning

Eating well is important at any time, but it is even more important when you are pregnant. The sooner you understand how to eat healthfully, the sooner you will be able to give your body—and, by extension, the fetus—the nutritional support it needs to grow a healthy baby.

Here are the basics that you should include:

- Four or more servings of fruits and vegetables.
- Four or more servings of whole-grain or enriched bread and cereal.
- Three or more servings of meat, poultry, fish, eggs, nuts, and dried beans or peas.

A single serving is:

- An eight-ounce cup of milk
- One ounce of cheese
- One slice of bread
- One ounce of cereal
- One-half to three-quarters of a cup of pasta
- One piece of fruit
- Eight ounces of juice
- Half a cup of cooked fruit
- Two or three ounces of meat, fish, or poultry
- One egg
- Three quarters of a cup of beans
- Two tablespoons of peanut butter
- One-quarter to one-half cup of nuts, sunflower, or sesame seeds

If you are not already eating healthfully, now is the time to start. But how? Experts tell us that it takes about 30 days to create new habits. You can lay the foundations of healthy eating throughout your pregnancy in the first month. Start by planning menus each week that include three balanced meals and several snacks. If you start now, by next month you'll be so used to your new, healthy manner of eating, it will take very little effort to stick to it!

Food Cravings and Intake

The National Research Council of the National Academy of Sciences, believes that you need to eat at least 300 more calories a day to support your growing fetus. Think of this as an extra bagel with cream cheese, an additional tuna fish sandwich, or 2 to $2^1/_2$ cups of low-fat milk. You don't really need to "eat for two," as the old saying suggested, but your recommended dietary allowances certainly do increase.

Meanwhile, food cravings and aversions to some foods are common. Just because you are ravenous doesn't mean that your body is actually nutritionally deficient. Feel like eating some pickled onions and ice cream? Fine. Just do it. However, keep in mind that almost anything you consume when you are expecting a baby can make its way to your baby via the placenta. You are your baby's source of food, so if you are craving only salty potato chips, think about adding other nutrients to this wish list. Aim for a variety of fresh, unprocessed foods.

- Cheeses, milks, and yogurt will give you calcium and proteins.
- Dark, green leafy vegetables will provide you with vitamin C, fiber, and folic acid.
- Lean red meats will give you iron and protein. Liver and poultry also are a good source of protein and iron, and so are fish such as flounder, tuna, salmon, or bluefish.
- Oranges can boost your vitamin C quotient and give you fiber, too.
- Are you hungry right now? Make a peanut butter sandwich on whole-grain bread.

Staying in Shape

The more physically fit you remain during pregnancy, the faster you will be able to return to your old shape after the baby is born. Exercise is also great for relieving stress and for increasing blood flow to the placenta nourishing your growing fetus.

Many women find that they are easily able to enjoy moderate exercise throughout pregnancy. Walking is fine, and an aerobics class may be just as acceptable. (Just don't take up hang gliding or rock climbing!) The important thing to remember is not to exercise to a point where you are tired or out of breath. Make sure you tell your teacher that you are pregnant. He or she may be able to adjust the regular routine to fit your needs. A certified exercise instructor should know how to troubleshoot for you while you are pregnant. For instance, exercises that pull on the abdominal muscles may have to be avoided. Sit-ups are an example. Jogging may not be well suited to pregnancy, especially in the second and third trimesters, because of the jarring effects of your heels hitting the ground and how stressful the motions can be on your joints and lower back. Speak with your doctor. Describe your athletic history in detail. Above all, use common sense. These nine months are not the time to begin any new fitness craze.

A Pregnant Pounds Primer

Not all the weight you gain will end up in your baby. Here's how a 25- to 30-pound weight gain breaks down:

- 4–6 lbs basically for you, stored in fat, protein, and other nutrients
- 2–3 lbs of increased fluids in your body
- 3–4 lbs of increased blood volume
- 1–2 lbs for enlarged breasts
- 2 lbs for enlarged uterus
- 6–8 lbs for your baby
- 2 lbs of amniotic fluid
- 1½ lbs of placenta, the tissue connecting you to your unborn baby, which handles all the feeding and cleansing

RECORD SHEET:
To Our Baby—A Welcome Message

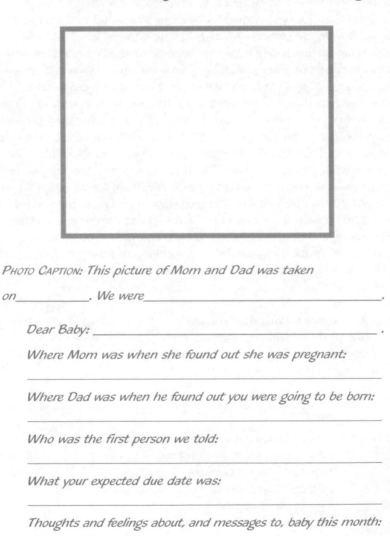

PHOTO CAPTION: This picture of Mom and Dad was taken

on_____. We were_____.

Dear Baby: _____ .

Where Mom was when she found out she was pregnant:

_____

Where Dad was when he found out you were going to be born:

_____

Who was the first person we told:

_____

What your expected due date was:

_____

Thoughts and feelings about, and messages to, baby this month:

_____

_____

Now is the time to . . .

Schedule a physical with your ob/gyn. Record it on the appropriate date in this planner!

Go to the appointment prepared. Draft a list of questions you have about pregnancy.

Get organized
You don't want to spend days looking for that 800 number for free referrals! Fortunately, *The Everything Pregnancy Organizer* has plenty of recordsheets (see the Appendix), so you can record all of the names, phone numbers, sources, suggestions, and other important items about pregnancy and childbirth. Use the pockets provided by the planner for small clippings.

Start taking photos of you as your body changes. We've provided a space at the end of each month for you to keep a visual diary.

The first day of your last period!

Dec 15

DAY 1

16

DAY 2

17

DAY 3

Scheduled Activities "To Do"	Important Reminders

DAY 4 — 18

DAY 5 — 19

DAY 6 — 20

Now is the time to . . .

Figure out your due date. Experts are usually uncertain about the exact date of fertilization; typically, due dates are predicted on the basis of the first day of your last period. Although timing the start of a pregnancy is an imprecise science, some couples have good hunches about when this new life began, based on their sex lives together. Couples who have been receiving medical help for fertility problems, may also have an exact date of fertilization.

Do your math
Obstetricians and childbirth specialists have a chart that makes predictions easy, especially if you've always had a regular twenty-eight-day menstrual cycle. However, here are two ways to check for a date on your own:

- Count 280 days from the first day of your last period. If that day was November 1, for instance, August 8 is your due date.

- Take the date of your last period, count three months back, and add seven days. For example, if your last period began on September 1, you would go back through August, July, and June. Then add seven days to come up with a due date of June 8.

Circle the big day in this planner!

Important Reminders	Scheduled Activities "To Do"

Now is the time to . . .

Start eating sensibly.
A balanced diet will help support a successful pregnancy. Make sure you consume adequate amounts of:

- Fresh fruits
- Vegetables
- Whole grains
- Lean proteins

Kick any unhealthy habits.
- Decrease caffeine.
- Eliminate alcohol.
- Stop smoking.

Ask your doctor for recommendations about vitamins.
It is important to give baby the best start by taking adequate amounts of nutrition. Prenatal supplements are helpful, preparing the body for a healthy pregnancy in advance. However, if you did not get on a prenatal supplementation plan, you can start taking supplements now. An especially important vitamin to be aware of is folic acid. Folic acid should be started about three months before a pregnancy because it helps prevent spinal abnormalities. You should continue taking it throughout the nine months.

21

22

23

DAY 7

DAY 8

DAY 9

DAY 10

24

DAY 11

25

DAY 12

26

Now is the time to . . .

Learn the lingo:
When you look at your chart in the doctor's office, you will see some medical terminology that may appear to be a foreign language. Because you are pregnant, you may see the term *gravida*, next to your name. It doesn't mean you are in a grave condition. *Gravida* simply means that you are a pregnant woman. If this is your first baby, you will be called a *primigravida*. *Multigravida* indicates that you have been pregnant before, even if the pregnancy ended in a miscarriage or abortion. *Para*, another foreign-looking term, means that you delivered a baby past the twentieth week of pregnancy.

Important Reminders	Scheduled Activities "To Do"

Important Reminders

Soon . . .

A momentous event may be occurring! But you may be unaware of it. You may be somewhere into your second or third week by the time that implantation of the egg into the womb occurs and unaware that such a momentous event is taking place. Some women do experience a bit of bleeding when this happens, though. However, anything more could be a cause for concern.

Be sure to see your doctor if you have:
- A positive pregnancy test
- Bleeding
- Pain
- Nausea
- Dizziness
- Severe cramps
- An unusual degree of fatigue

These are the signs of an ectopic pregnancy, a potentially life-threatening situation. Seek emergency treatment immediately.

Scheduled Activities "To Do"

27 conception

DAY 13

28

DAY 14

29

DAY 15

Scheduled Activities "To Do"	Important Reminders

DAY 16

30

DAY 17

31

DAY 18

Jan 1

Dietary requirements during pregnancy.
Here's a chart of exactly how much more you need now that you are pregnant. The percentage refers to the increase over what you used to eat before becoming pregnant:

Overall Calories = 14% more
Protein = 20% more
Vitamin D = 100% more
Vitamin E = 25% more
Vitamin K = 8% more
Vitamin C = 17% more
Thiamin = 36% more
Riboflavin = 23% more
Niacin = 13% more
Vitamin B6 = 27% more
Folate = 122% more
Vitamin B12 = 10% more
Calcium = 50% more
Phosphorus = 50% more
Magnesium = 14% more
Iron = 100% more
Zinc = 100% more
Iodine = 17% more
Selenium = 18% more

Important Reminders	Scheduled Activities "To Do"

Now is the time to . . .

**Allow yourself
regular leisure time.**
If you think of your time as scarce
or as precious money to spend,
you will feel fragmented trying to
use it wisely. Leisure time is a
necessity now, not a reward for
having completed everything.
Deep benefits for both you and
your unborn baby come from
forgetting your chores and what
time it is. Take a magazine into
the bathroom, fill the tub, climb
in, and relax. Such a leisurely
soak will give you the strength to
do more later. Besides, you may
not have many opportunities for
such a luxury after the baby is
born.

Did you know that . . .
The heart rate of your baby-to-be
starts off very rapidly, at about
180 beats a minute, and through
the pregnancy, it declines to about
140 as the baby's system
becomes more complex. When
you are forming small capillaries,
those blood vessels impede the
blood so the baby can pick up
more oxygen and the heart doesn't
have to beat as fast. Pumping
blood through the developing
systems, this heart may be the
clue you are waiting to hear in one
of your upcoming doctor's visits.

DAY 19

DAY 20

DAY 21

Scheduled Activities "To Do"	Important Reminders

DAY 22

30 5

Now is the time to . . .

Start making a habit of recording your thoughts for posterity. Make time right now to write down what you're thinking and feeling at this very special time in your life!

  Use this organizer and calendar as the perfect spot for your journal.

DAY 23

31 6

DAY 24

X 7

28

Symptoms of pregnancy are . . .

Everyone is different, but in the first weeks after conception there are early signs of pregnancy that are quite predictable. Changes to watch for include:

- You missed your period. If your menstrual cycle is normally irregular, you are under a lot of stress, or feeling sick, this may not be a dependable signal. It is also possible to have a light, bloody discharge and still be pregnant. Some experts say that up to 22 percent of all expectant women report some bleeding early on.
- Your breasts are sore, enlarged, and/or extra sensitive to touch.
- You are nauseous. "Morning sickness," a classic sign of pregnancy, can happen any time of day.
- You are exhausted and sleepy. Fatigue is a predictable signal of early pregnancy.
- You need to urinate frequently.
- You feel faint or a little dizzy.
- You have an achy, heavy sensation in your pelvis.
- You've become intensely emotional (thanks to hormonal changes!).
- Your taste buds have changed. Some women suddenly develop a strong distaste for alcohol, coffee, and cigarette smoke and complain of a metallic sensation in their mouths. Others begin to crave particular foods.

8 2

9 8

Missed period   10 8

DAY 25

DAY 26

DAY 27

Scheduled Activities "To Do"	Important Reminders
DAY 28	***Now is the time***
8 11	***to . . . miss your period!***
	Until now, you haven't even missed your period yet. In fact, that rich, spongy lining in your uterus, which served the implantation adventure quite well, is what would have been shed during regular monthly menstruation. Because you have an embryo growing, changing, and manufacturing profound changes in your womb, you miss this monthly event, experiencing one of the first clear signs of pregnancy. The embryo is secreting a hormone, known as human chorionic gonadotropin (HCG), into your blood stream, which interferes with menstruation. This is the hormone that appears in your urine on a pregnancy test and alerts you to the news of a new life beginning.
DAY 29	
6 12	
DAY 30/31	
7+8 13+14	
0	

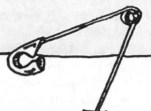

MONTH TWO

Creative napping, Trying to picture an embryo, Opening windows everywhere—ahhh, fresh air! Exercising mystery muscles on your pelvic floor.

TO DO THIS MONTH

- ☐ *Nap.*
- ☐ *Treat yourself like a queen.*
- ☐ *Read about your unborn baby.*
- ☐ *List your symptoms.*
- ☐ *Cut out fried foods.*
- ☐ *Learn Kegel exercises.*
- ☐ *Look at your clothes and start planning ahead.*
- ☐ *Stay away from smokers.*

Welcome to month two of your pregnancy! Can you imagine a time more filled with secret joy, hold-your-breath anxiety, and dramatic shifts away from what had been your normal, everyday existence? Where life once revolved around you, and perhaps your mate, now it has become more complicated. You, in fact, are no longer yourself. You are thinking and actually living for two, and one of this pair has yet to be born. Yet, in reality, there has never been a more important time to assess your own needs and realize just how important they are. Slow down. Take it easy. Be kind to yourself. Racing through life, trying to get it all done, all finished, all ready, everyday, all day long, is not the answer. You'll drive yourself nuts. Get used to a brand-new lifestyle: Perhaps for the first time in decades, nap is an important three letter word for you right now. With the mandate to take more time for yourself in mind, consider:

- *Assessing your current lifestyle, listing any changes to make that will help you through pregnancy.* For example, do you regularly attend "Happy Hours" after work? Think about cutting back on activities that will expose you to second-hand smoke and encourage you to drink. Maybe that "Happy Hour" is better spent taking a nap!

- *Scheduling time each week for you and your spouse to "date."* You won't have a lot of one-on-one time after the baby is born, so make it a point to enjoy the time you have alone together over the next few months. Perhaps you can even get in a couple of weekend getaways to a bed and breakfast. You won't want to fly during your pregnancy, and travelling with a newborn is a challenge. Try to get in at least one last "vacation" together while you have the chance, even if it's only to the tourist spot nearest your hometown.

- *Scheduling time for regular beauty treatments.* It's time to treat yourself like a queen. Though many women are thrilled to be pregnant, they can feel self-conscious about the changes in their appearance during pregnancy. For example, many women gain weight and start to lose some hair. Later,

after the baby's born, they may find long hair imprac-
tical (babies love to pull mom's hair, just for fun!).
Scheduling regular manicures, pedicures, and haircuts
can help you maintain a positive attitude about your appearance throughout your nine months. Also, chances are you'll
have little time for such indulgences after the baby is born,
so it's doubly important to enjoy yourself now.

This Month's Priorities

❏ Read about your unborn baby.
❏ Continue to record your symptoms.
❏ Learn Kegel exercises.
❏ Learn how to nap.
❏ Look at your clothes and start planning ahead for your
    maternity wardrobe.

How Your Baby Grows

At the beginning of the second month, your embryo, which is
embedded in the side of your uterus, may be no larger than a
grape. During this month, your baby's brain grows rapidly. The right
and left hemispheres are formed and cranial nerves
branch out. Membranes appear around the brain and
fluid protects the tiny mass of cells. By the end of
this month, the brain is working and exerting its
influence on the way the unborn child moves.

At about week seven of development, a face
is beginning to be discernible, but eyes, apparent because of a black pigment beneath the
skin, are on the sides of the head and closely
sealed. A recognizable face appears with a little
nose, and the jaw moves into place to make way
for a mouth. The tongue isn't far behind. Later in the month, the
eyes shift from the sides to the front of the face. Tissues from either

side come together to form the face and nose and the buds of twenty baby teeth can be seen by experts. Inside the ears, the parts of the body responsible for hearing and equilibrium grow.

A heart has begun to circulate blood through the tiny body and signs of a nearly completed nervous system can be seen. Although the lungs, intestines, liver, and kidneys are not yet fully formed, important internal organ systems are nearly completed by the end of this second month. Heart chambers form and the heartbeat becomes very human in pattern. Lungs enlarge. Bones develop. The digestive and circulatory systems keep growing. Although your fetus is not really eating anything in a digestive sense, the stomach is already secreting gastric juices. The liver also is manufacturing blood cells for bone marrow.

At eight weeks, the embryo can be called a fetus, which simply means "young one."

Your unborn baby will have grown to the size of a plump strawberry. Arms and legs are clearly in place but at the ends of each, the embryo has only little clefts, which will soon turn into hands, fingers, feet, and toes. Soon, these little feet will begin to kick. Muscles, which have also been forming, start exercising just as they will in the outside world. Although you probably can't feel anything yet, your baby begins to move around inside his or her safe watery world. These first fetal movements are often called quickening. However, most expectant moms don't become sensitive to these flutterings until about the eighteenth to twentieth week of pregnancy.

By the end of the second month, the fetus has grown 240 times in length and a million, yes a million, times in weight.

What You Can Expect to Experience
Emotional Changes

"From the very first positive news on your pregnancy test to childbirth, there is a tremendous force, a tremendous environmental drive subverting your individuality," says Sanford Matthews, M.D. "It can be a perfectly wonderful experience—and it often is—but it can also be a perplexing time when nothing is grounded, not even the size of your ring finger."

"The hormones being marshaled to protect and nurture your pregnancy affect your brain," continues Matthews. "You may experience what he calls "a chemical brainwash."

The same hormones that affect your mood can affect you physically, producing sometimes uncomfortable physical changes. In turn, bodily discomfort can affect your psychological well-being on a day-to-day basis. It seems like a vicious cycle at times. Fortunately, for many women, the aches, pains, and upsets present during the first trimester ease up later in the pregnancy. The best way to handle the subtle and not-so-subtle physical changes may be to anticipate them as predictable and quite normal.

Physical Changes

- Your vagina feels full, congested, and actually bigger than it used to be. You may also have more secretions. An increase in the amount of clear or white mucus is normal unless you are sore. If that happens, let your doctor know right away because you may have developed an infection. Report any itching, pain, or colored or foul-smelling discharge.
- Your breasts are growing. The areolas, the pigmented areas around the nipple, also are getting bigger and darker in color. Veins in your breast are more noticeable and could be painful, sensitive, or actually throbbing, especially when in contact with a tight bra or any pressure.
- Your need for oxygen increases. You may feel the need to open windows for some fresh air.
- Faintness or dizziness can occur occasionally because your blood pressure is lower than it used to be. Fainting can also be caused by low blood sugar or not enough iron.

Nausea, or Morning Sickness

Morning sickness may be one of the very first signals of pregnancy, first mentioned by ancient Egyptians as long ago as 2000 B.C.

Morning sickness affects about 50 percent of all pregnant women, and it doesn't just occur in the morning, either. An upset stomach and outright vomiting can happen at any particular time of day, making us all wonder why it isn't called all-day sickness.

No one knows exactly why some women feel sick while others appear to bounce through the day eating everything in sight. The cause of morning sickness may likely be the level of HCG (human chorionic gonadotropin) or the pregnancy hormone in the blood. HCG rises a few days after a missed period, which is when morning sickness usually starts. Continuously secreted by the brain and the placenta, HCG peaks at about eight weeks and dramatically falls at about twelve weeks, when a woman who has been sick and vomiting for months suddenly awakens with barely a discomfort. This twelve-week limit doesn't always hold true for everyone, however. The National Institutes of Health (NIH) studied 8,000 pregnant women in two separate surveys done during the 1980s and reported that not only were 29 percent nauseous up to week 16, but 25 percent also were getting sick well into their twentieth week.

Another theory is that you are more likely to be nauseous if your fertilized ovum came from your right ovary. As odd as it may seem, here's the explanation behind this idea: You have an important ovarian vein that carries hormones from the ovary directly to your liver on the right side. The theory is that having your unborn baby originate on this right side brings on a kind of hormonal overload, delivering an extra wallop to your liver and making you sick. In research completed in 1986, women whose eggs had been released from the left side were less likely to have nausea.

Whatever the theory, morning sickness appears to be triggered by the smell of certain foods, odors, or the smoke from a lit cigarette. It usually is worse for first-time moms-to-be. Studies indicate that you are also more likely to feel sick if you:

♂ are under age twenty.
♂ weigh more than 170 pounds.
♂ are having twins.
♂ are a nonsmoker.

The extent of your morning sickness can run the gamut, from a case of mild queasiness during the first twelve weeks to severe vomiting for nine long months.

There are dramatic cases when expectant mothers vomit almost continually throughout pregnancy. Only a small percentage of women experience this condition, called *hyperemesis gravidarum*. Some unfortunate moms-to-be throw up so continually and so violently, hospitalization and intravenous feeding are required to bring symptoms under control and restore the mother's biochemistry.

Morning Sickness Solutions

Simply knowing why you feel sick is probably of little comfort. What you need are ideas to calm your stomach. Here are ways to combat morning sickness; these are collected from ex-pregnant women as well as pregnancy experts.

♂ Try eating dry crackers, toast, or fruit. If you actually do feel sickest in the morning, keep a box of crackers by the side of your bed, and eat something as soon as you wake up.
♂ Eliminate fried or highly seasoned foods.
♂ Go with many mini-meals instead of three big square meals a day.
♂ Drink lots of water but not with foods. Wait at least thirty minutes before or after eating to take a drink.
♂ Stick with beverages that are either very hot or very cold. If liquids of any kind are treating your stomach unkindly, get your share via fruits and vegetables. Eat lettuce, for instance. It's mostly water.
♂ Try fruit sorbets, ice cream, yogurt, or milk shakes.

- Even when you don't feel like eating, force yourself. An empty stomach can make you even more queasy than one partially filled.
- Complex carbohydrates may go down easier than other foods. Along with crackers and toast, nibble on dry cereal, bread sticks, rice cakes, plain popcorn (skip the butter), and baked potatoes.
- Some expectant moms praise the power of proteins; hard-boiled eggs and cheese are wiser choices than red meat.
- Steer clear of smells that can trigger occasions of nausea if you can. For instance, if the scent of freshly brewing coffee sets your stomach rolling, ask your mate to pick up his cup of java on the outside. When you have to cook, open the kitchen windows or turn on an exhaust fan.
- Prenatal vitamins, which contain iron, can irritate your digestive tract. If you are experiencing serious bouts of morning sickness, speak with your doctor about altering your vitamins or even taking a vacation from your vitamin regimen.
- The B vitamins taken as supplements, as well as foods rich in them can help, according to Dr. Lauerson. Check with your own doctor, but consider taking a B complex and B6.
- Move slowly. Aim for tranquillity. Sit on the side of your bed for a few minutes each morning. Let your stomach settle before you attempt any quick moves.
- Ask your doctor about medications, especially if you are so sick that you are worried about your unborn baby. New, anti-emetic drugs can be used under the care of a doctor. Emetrol, a mint-flavored liquid, is available in pharmacies over-the-counter. Maalox, and other antacids, may be able to relieve symptoms, too. Antihistamines have also been known to quiet queasy stomachs. However, do not take anything without the backing of your doctor. Always ask first.

Constipation Cures

Constipation affects many pregnant women, and, what's worse, it can lead to troublesome hemorrhoids. Progesterone, one of the hormones now circulating wildly in your system, relaxes the gastrointestinal muscles in the walls of your intestines and slows down bowel movements. If you are constipated, you are not alone. More than half of all expectant mothers suffer from constipation at some point during their pregnancies.

To combat it without resorting to laxatives, try the following:

- Drinking lots of water—up to ten or twelve eight-ounce glasses a day. The increase in fluids should make your gastrointestinal tract feel better.
- Try eating fiber-rich foods, such as prunes, figs, whole fruits and vegetables, including the skins or peels, seeds, and whole-grain breads or cereals with bran. They work as natural laxatives. Fruit juices also help.
- Check out your vitamins. A common side effect of iron supplementation is constipation, and some brands even have stool softeners to counteract the problem of constipation. Different brands also contain varying concentrations of vitamins and minerals, so if one particular manufacturer's blend upsets your system, try another.
- Stay active. If you've stopped or slowed up your exercise routine because you are pregnant, this lack of movement could be aggravating your constipation problem. Go for a 20-minute walk at least once a day.
- If constipation has become such a nightmare for you that you are developing hemorrhoids, speak with your doctor.

Gas and Bloating

Stomach rumbling, burping, a feeling of fullness, and the overwhelming urge to pass gas in the most embarrassing situations are just a few of the symptoms pregnant women have to endure. Eating a fiber-rich diet, often recommended in pregnancy, can also cause bloating and gas until your body adjusts to this new diet. Here are some things to try:

- Gas-X, a simethecone-based supplement designed to combat gas (but ask your doctor first).
- Stick to small meals because they won't overload your digestive tract.
- Eat slowly, and don't gulp down anything, especially carbonated drinks.
- Take yoga. Anxiety alone can work your body up to a frenzy. But—don't forget to tell the instructor that you are pregnant.

Also, check out your diet with your doctor. You may want to reduce or eliminate some of the foods that are known to produce gas—at least until your stomach settles. They include:

- Apples
- Bananas
- Beans
- Broccoli
- Cabbage
- Cauliflower
- Corn
- Cucumbers
- Meringues
- Milk
- Oats and other high-fiber grains
- Onions
- Turnips

Exhaustion

Fatigue is caused by hormones, especially progesterone—the culprit for quite a few of these meddlesome side effects of pregnancy. Even when researchers inject this hormone into laboratory animals in experiments, the subjects become extremely sleepy. Give in to the feeling, and take a nap if you can. Keep in mind that you are giving your unborn baby a peaceful growing environment. Physicians believe that extreme tiredness is a way of forcing you to rest.

Frequent Urination

Do you need to urinate frequently, and sometimes all night long? You might have a urinary tract infection, which can lead to premature labor, so speak with your doctor about your symptoms. However, early in pregnancy, frequent urination can be caused by progesterone relaxing the muscles in your bladder. The nerves that direct the need to go to the bathroom are also sending signals to your brain even though you may have just recently urinated.

If nightly trips out of bed are ruining your sleep,

- Drink less in the evenings.
- Practice Kegel excercises for improved bladder control (see "Taking Care of Yourself," below).
- Empty your bladder completely every time you go to the bathroom. Think you are finished? Sit still for a second. Try to go again.

Taking Care of Yourself

Maintaining Pelvic Muscle Tone

The hammock of muscles that support your bowel, bladder, and womb on the floor of your pelvis needs to stay strong and elastic. When you are pregnant, these muscles get softer and spongier. When you add this to the weight of your growing baby directly above, you can end up with a problem. You feel heavy and uncomfortable. When you sneeze, laugh, or cough suddenly, you may even end up leaking a bit of urine.

Pelvic floor excercises help improve bladder control and also are great for labor, delivery, and helping you recover faster after the baby is born.

You can do pelvic floor exercises—known as Kegel exercises—anytime, anywhere. Build up to doing them as much as one hundred times a day, but not all at once. Known as Kegel exercises, they can be done at your convenience, and no one even really needs to know you are exercising. Do them while watching television, riding in a car, combing your hair, or before climbing out of bed in the morning. The goal is to improve your ability to tighten the muscles surrounding the vagina and perineum (pelvic floor). Here's how:

- With your legs slightly apart, tighten and release the muscles around your vagina. There are two techniques to help you figure out how to do this. First, put your hand over your pubic bones and contract your vaginal muscles up to your fingers. Do this five, ten, twenty times. Work your way up to one hundred a day.
- The next time you are going to the bathroom, stop the flow of urine right in the middle. Then start again. Then stop again.
- Tighten the muscles of the buttocks, as though trying to prevent the escape of feces. (This same group of muscles is used to stop the flow of urine.)
- Tighten and release your vaginal muscles, but take a slower approach. In fact, as you tighten, count to six. As you release, count to four. Tighten to six. Relax to four. Breathe normally and resist that temptation to hold your breath.

Napping Regularly

Although napping is never going to be a substitute for a good night's sleep, a nap a day is a necessity for many pregnant women—and certainly will benefit your unborn baby.

- If you can't carve out hours of free time, steal five, ten, or just fifteen minutes from your busy day and close your eyes.
- Opt for something you can stretch out on—a bed or couch instead of a chair.

- Don't fall asleep when you're stuffed (after a big meal) or starved (with a stomach growling for food).
- Set the room temperature for the mid-sixties. If you are too hot or too cold, you won't be able to drift off.
- Watch your caffeine consumption.
- Let go of anxieties. Tell yourself that you can find the answers later, when you wake up.
- Develop a nap ritual. One woman, who worked full time in an office until the day before her baby was born, took an exercise mat to work so she could roll it out in the afternoon and close her eyes. If you have an office door to close out the world, do so. If that's not possible, and you can't even find space to stretch out, settle for a catnap. Just close your eyes and rest.

Energy Boosters

- Most people start to slump after twelve hours of being awake. You can blame sleepiness on being pregnant, of course, but if you are trying to push yourself through a long day of unending activity, you can also blame it on your body rhythms.
- Drink water when you feel fatigued. Your brain is 75 percent water, and every chemical reaction that occurs in your body uses water. If you are dehydrated, you will be less productive.
- Don't slouch. Good posture—neck lengthened, chin in, shoulders back, head up—can actually give you 30 percent more lung capacity.
- Stay away from sweets. Sugars offer an instant pick-up, but your body will droop as soon as the extra insulin is churned out.

Thinking Fit

If you have never picked up a weight in your life or purchased a pair of walking shoes, don't be discouraged to start now.

Food Reaction Worksheet

1. Foods that make me queasy:

   _____

   _____

   _____

   _____

   _____

   _____

2. Foods that relieve nausea:

   _____

   _____

   _____

   _____

   _____

   _____

3. Strange but true cravings:

   _____

   _____

   _____

   _____

   _____

   _____

Pregnancy may be the perfect time to become more conscious of just what your body is capable of doing.

Finding and sticking to an exercise routine can help you overcome many of the common problems of pregnancy: backaches, loss of urinary control, hemorrhoids, discomfort during sex, poor posture, muscle stiffness, and lack of energy. Activity will increase your flexibility and make it easier for you to adjust your balance through all the phases and stages of pregnancy.

Research conducted by Jennifer Lovejoy, a physiological psychologist at the Women's Health Research Program at the Pennington Biomedical Research Center at Louisiana State University, found that many women who find themselves out of shape and overweight later in life blame pregnancy for the turning point in their metabolism. Sure, there are good reasons to blame this life-changing event. Great reasons, in fact: hormonal changes, new eating habits, stress, and no time or energy for exercise. Yet, pregnancy does not have to leave you with a legacy of twenty extra pounds. Lovejoy found that psychological factors played a key part in taking your body through a year of wild transformation. The secret may be exercise. By making exercise as much of a part of your routine as brushing your teeth or combing your hair, you stand a better chance of staying in touch with your body through all the ups, downs, ins, and outs.

So think fit. Don't worry about thin. Consider yourself voluptuous, but keep on moving. Walk. Move. Take a few minutes a day to stretch and bend. You deserve it.

Before You Exercise

Before you begin any new exercise program or aerobic dancing class, hire a personal trainer, or follow your good friends onto the tennis court, check with your practitioner. Even if the sessions are designed for expectant or postpartum moms, you should still run the idea by your practitioner first.

Exercising moderately throughout your pregnancy, especially in the first trimester, is going to make you feel great and remain strong. Unlike later trimesters, where added weight can throw you off balance, in the first trimester, your pregnant body is less apt to feel awkward. Moderation still should be your mantra, however.

Certain activities—rollerblading and ice skating—are probably best avoided. Your ligaments actually relax when you are expecting, so knee, ankle, and foot injuries are more likely. Be wary of any high-impact sports. If you've been playing tennis, for instance, you might want to avoid competitive singles games and switch to doubles.

Another danger is *hyperthermia*, or elevated body temperature. Long-distance and marathon running can raise body temperatures to a dangerous level, as can other sports. "If you play indoor hand-ball, paddleball, or racquetball during the first trimester, be aware of the fact that these courts are rarely well-ventilated and pose a threat of hyperthermia," explains Howard Shapiro, M.D., a Connecticut obstetrician-gynecologist and author. Such strenuous exercise in the first trimester has been associated with birth defects, and later in pregnancy the stress shifts your blood away from your uterus to your legs, possibly decreasing the oxygen being carried to your unborn baby. When you raise your body's tempera-ture for a prolonged time, especially during the third, fourth, and fifth weeks of pregnancy, experts suspect that you can cause dam-age to the developing fetus's brain, skull, and spinal cord. Simply having a high fever because you are ill doesn't appear to be as damaging as raising your body temperature during a long physical workout. If you have been a marathon runner, you might want to know that your core body temperature can actually rise an average of 34.7 degrees Fahrenheit during a long race, according to Shapiro. No race is worth the danger. Other sports to put on hold are water-skiing, scuba diving, horseback riding, basketball, gymnas-tics, field hockey, jumping rope, and softball.

The best exercises are those that are low impact and aerobic, such as walking, cycling, and swimming. Limit sessions to thirty min-utes. Although bowling, volleyball, and softball don't offer as much aerobic benefit, you can play safely when pregnant, according to Shapiro. The continuous jumping in volleyball is not great for your joints and ligaments, however. Golf, too, is an activity that should stay on your list of things to do, even though you shouldn't "expect to improve your golf swing" after the fifth month, when you have to compensate for "an increasing abdominal enlargement."

However, explains Shapiro, "If a woman is aerobically fit prior to pregnancy and exercises prudently under climate-controlled conditions, hyperthermia during pregnancy can be avoided."

"In reality, any exercises that you have been doing all along in your life are going to be fine during pregnancy," says Howard Berk, M.D.

Just don't push it—now is not the time to become a triathlete overnight!

Exercise Dos and Don'ts

Do stop moving
- Before you become utterly exhausted.
- If you feel pain.
- If you are short of breath.

Don't ever
- Exercise without drinking water before, during, and afterward.
- Jump up suddenly.
- Try an exercise movement that requires you to lie flat on your back after you are twenty weeks' pregnant.
- Dive into a routine without warming up with some slow steady movements first.

Gearing up

Find something to wear that won't make you want to cringe in front of the mirror, classmates, or your family members. Gear to get you going is more important than you might think because when you are feeling sluggish, you'll use any excuse not to move your body. Not having comfortable clothes can become a big hurdle. A comfortable, support-ive bra is especially important. Nonrestrictive clothes will also let your body air out and breathe when you warm up. You don't have to think in terms of high fashion. Cotton sweats, shorts, your husband's T-shirts, a leotard in a larger size than you might ordinarily wear will all do just fine.

You may also want to purchase an exercise mat to use when exercising at home. Some moms find a carpeted floor just fine. Others want the cushion of a big, soft pillow or want to be up against a wall or something firm for back support. A towel often comes in handy, too.

An Exercise Program at-a-Glance

Warming Up

Stand Tall

Place your feet slightly more than shoulder-width apart, keep your knees soft, and drop your arms to your sides. Tuck your backside under. Square your shoulders back and tilt your pelvis slightly forward so your tail bone points down. Breathe slowly, deeply, calmly. Breathe in through your nose and push your head toward the ceiling, elongating your spine at the same time. Now, breathe out and reach out with your arms, up toward the ceiling. Repeat three to four times.

Swing

With your arms limp and relaxed at your sides, breathe in and out slowly. Now, swing your arms in, crossing them in front and then out to shoulder level. Repeat three to four times.

Make Circles

Increase the muscle tension in your arms a little. Keeping your elbows soft and your hands relaxed, circle your arms in toward the midpoint of your body, crossing them in front and then going up and out as if you were drawing large circles with your arms going in an inward direction. Repeat three times. Now reverse the direction and make three large circles in an outward direction.

Note: These swings and circles should make your arms and upper body feel energized.

Stretch Your Upper Back

Still standing, keep your feet slightly more than shoulder-width apart, your weight as evenly distributed as possible given your stage of pregnancy, your knees soft, and your arms at your sides. Lift your arms out to the sides to approximately shoulder level, inhaling as you lift. Exhale and slowly bring your extended arms forward at chest level, leaning slightly forward as you do and letting your pelvis tilt in just a bit. You should feel the stretch through your upper and middle back. Now, return your arms to your sides at shoulder level and contract the back muscles between your shoulder blades as you do. Exhale and repeat this stretch three or four times.

Roll Your Shoulders

Try to breathe naturally through this movement. You may be shocked by how much tension you discover in your shoulder and neck. Bring your shoulders up toward your ears and then backward in a fluid, rolling motion. Try to visualize drawing circles with your shoulders. Repeat three times. Now, reverse the movement, bringing your shoulders up and then forward. Repeat three times.

Stretch Like a Cat

Before you get tired of being on your feet, try this standing-up cat stretch to stretch and strengthen your lower back. Lower your body into a semi-sitting position with your hands on your thighs to support your weight. Bend your knees and lean a little forward with your upper body. Slowly roll up through the back, one vertebra at a time, beginning with the lowest one and continuing up through your mid- and upper back. Your back should actually be curved like a shallow C. Your head should be aligned with your neck. Hold this stretch for a minute or two and then slowly roll back down to your semi-sitting position. Inhale when you curve up and exhale as you roll down.

Squat

Squatting is a great exercise for preparing your perineum for delivery. Keep your back straight, open your legs, and move down.

If you need a chair for support the first few times, grab the seat with both hands to steady yourself. Turn your feet out slightly and try to keep your heels flat on the floor. You may even want to roll up a towel or mat to put under your heels at first. You are stretching your inner thighs, and you can increase the stretch by placing your elbows on top and pushing down very gently. Clasp your hands in front of you and try to hold this position for as long as you can.

Squatting loosens your pelvic joints while it strengthens your back and thigh muscles. A lot of squatting during the nine months leading up to delivery can actually protect your back and will ease back pain. As your baby grows bigger and bigger, just let your uterus rest right between your stretched-out thighs. Lengthen your back. Imagine a string pulling the very top of your head up to the ceiling.

Sit to Stretch and Ease Strain

First, try sitting down on a mat or padded surface. With your legs in front of you, knees bent, and feet flat on the floor, clasp your hands in front of you. Keeping your arms straight, twist first to the left and then to the right of your bent knees. You'll be turning your shoulders to the right and then to the left and touching your clasped fingers to one side of your thighs and then to the other. An easy stretch, this movement actually strengthens the muscles of your back, hips, and abdomen, according to the American College of Obstetricians and Gynecologists (ACOG).

Cross Your Legs

Still seated, try crossing your legs in front of your body now in what is known as the semi-lotus position. Sit up as tall as you can. Put your hand under one backside cheek and lift it up and out. Then, reposition the other cheek as well so you are sitting squarely.

Rest your hands on your knees easily. Relax. Breathe slowly
in and out. Twist your body first to the right, allowing your left
hand to grab your right knee as you move. Your right hand will
move out to the right side and rest on the floor or mat to hold
you steady during this trunk twist. Turn your head completely to the
right and look around behind you. Change directions now.

Reach Out

Still kneeling up on all fours, exhale and stretch your right hand
forward while your left leg moves straight out in back. Feel them pull
away from your body in either direction. You may lose your balance,
so take this slowly. Push back with your heel flat while your toes
remain pointed down. Stretch. Reach with your fingertips. Let your
head hang loose. Bring hand and foot back in and relax. Do the
other side, exhaling before each lift.

Ease Neck Strain

Stay seated and make sure your legs are comfortable. You don't
want to cut off any circulation, so move a little if you feel your
blood flow is being cut down even in the slightest. Let your knees
flop outward and pull your legs in. Grab your ankles and put the
soles of your feet together. Tilt your chin to your chest and clasp
your hands at the back of your head with your elbows out. Press
the back of your head toward your clasped hands.

Now, lift your chin so that your eyes are level and forward.
Place your right hand on the top of your head and extend your left
arm out to the side about eight to twelve inches from your body.
Tilt your head toward the right. Your right ear is heading toward
your right shoulder. Reach out with your left arm. Keep your eyes
and your chin facing forward. Hold the position for up to ten seconds and breathe naturally. Repeat the movement on the other side.

Tailor Sit

Stay seated: with your back straight and your head held high,
grab your ankles and bring the soles of your feet together directly in
front of you. Pull your feet in as close to your body as you can.

Your body is going to be more supple when you are pregnant because of the hormones circulating that are relaxing all your joints and ligaments, so this position may be easier than ever before in your life. Take hold of your ankles in this position and place your elbows and arms on your inner thighs. Press down slightly with your arms so that you push your thighs open wider.

Kneel Up and Stretch Out

Kneel up on your hands and knees. Make sure that your knees are about ten inches apart and your hands are just under your shoulders. You want to create the effect of a steady, sturdy table with your kneeling body and flat back. Keep your spine straight from head to tailbone as you begin. Now, curl your back up just as a cat might do when angry. Stretch way up and let your head drop between your shoulders. Now, let your spine slowly curl back down and lift your chin and head up in the opposite direction. In a rocking motion, repeat three or four times.

Twist Like a Cat

Stay in the kneeling position: try twisting from side to side, moving your head around to look at your heels, first to the left and then to the right. Exhale and turn back to the center. Inhale and twist in the opposite direction. Rest back and breathe deeply.

Sit Back on Your Heels and Reach Out . . . Relax

While you are still on the floor on all fours, slowly begin to sit back on your heels, curling your backside down until it is resting on the back of your calves. Tuck your head down and face into your bent knees while you stretch your arms out straight along the floor in front of you. Breathe in and out slowly. Reach out with your fingertips. Relax. Your belly should be resting easily between your thighs. Hold this stretched-out position for a few minutes before curling back up on all fours. Repeat three or four times.

Exercise Worksheet

Type of Exercise: _____

_____

_____

_____

_____

Time of Day: _____

_____

Duration: _____

_____

How I Felt After: _____

_____

_____

_____

_____

_____

_____

_____

_____

_____

_____

_____

_____

_____

_____

_____

_____

Tone Your Pelvis

Kneel with your elbows on the floor, your chin resting on your hands, and your buttocks up in the air. This kind of knee-to-chest position allows your uterus to fall away from its pressing position on the pelvic floor. With your knees spread and your head still quietly resting on your crossed arms, tighten the muscles along your vagina and your rectum. Contract for a few seconds and then release. Repeat three to four times.

Put Your Back Against a Wall

Although it sounds easy, this exercise actually takes some stamina and will help strengthen your back, torso, and upper body. Stand with your upper back leaning against a smooth wall while your feet are firmly planted but about ten to twelve inches out. Lean the lower section of your spine into the wall. You'll feel the stress in your thighs. But do push back. Hold the position and count to ten. Rest. Repeat ten times.

Lift Your Legs

Start out by kneeling on all fours once again. Your hands should be just beneath your shoulders for support. Knees are about ten inches apart. Keeping your hands flat and firmly planted on the floor or mat, lift your left knee and foot together in one motion out to the side of your body and then down again. You'll be trying to redistribute your weight so your arms remain steady and the right side of your body is still during these swings. Next, lift this bent left leg out to the back and drop it down to touch lightly on the mat. Use your hip to make this movement. Keep your spine steady. Lift to the side and back again. Repeat three to four times. Then, work your right leg in the same way.

Looking Good

Words from Wise Women

"You've got to try hard not to feel dumpy or let yourself look like a slob even if you aren't reporting to a job during your pregnancy."
— J. S., a former systems analyst
pregnant for the second time

"This is my first pregnancy and I'm dressing to please myself as much as for anyone else. It's so important for my self-esteem."
— S. S., psychotherapist
who went back to school
for a business degree

"Near the end of my first trimester, I would get up in the morning and end up trying on ten different outfits before I found one that snapped, buttoned or didn't fit skintight."
— S. D., a nurse

"When my mother was pregnant, she wore a lot of black. She tells me that she was happy to have become pregnant in the late fifties because that was the turning point from dowdy to delightful. The elastic panel was in, drawstring tops had arrived, and she was able to bypass the potato sacks they had been trying to pass off on pregnant women."
— M. F., a former
fashion buyer's assistant

"Even though something might look ridiculous on a hanger, try it on. This is the one stage of your life when you can't trust those old clothing instincts you thought you had narrowed down. Seriously, I never believed that an extra long sweater with matching leg warmers would look anything but ridiculous on a pregnant me. Yet, believe me, I wore it and received compliments."
— B. V., full-time mom

Maternity Chic

In times past, the pregnant woman had few options for looking glamorous, smartly dressed for business, or even comfortably outfitted for a casual lifestyle. Fortunately, all that has changed. Today, pregnant women have a plethora of options in maternity dress colors, cuts, textiles, and design details.

A common misconception is to base maternity wardrobe recommendations on two-season thinking. You are told that you fall into either spring–summer or autumn–winter. Well, anyone who has ever been pregnant will intimately understand the fallacy of such thinking. If you are due in October, you can't buy clothes with a fall mentality. What about those hot July and August days of summer when you are very much pregnant? An October due date puts you right in the middle of three seasons, especially if you live in a Northern or Middle-Atlantic state where weather patterns run the gamut. Even if you live in Southern California or the southernmost tip of Florida, it may be helpful to know what lies ahead when it comes to getting dressed in the morning.

Dressing Basics

Your lifestyle will dictate what kind of clothes you need to have in your closet in the months to come. If you are a lawyer working full time and expected to appear in court, then you'll be thinking suits. However, if you are a full-time, at-home mother, you'll be interested in more casual clothes. Here are some basic guidelines, based on due dates.

Clothes Shopping Checklist

If You Are Due in January or February
You will outgrow your waistband by August–September.
You'll need:

- ❏ Dresses
    - ❏ 1 casual. Consider a jumper that can be dressed up or down and in a color that won't be out of place in either early September or all the way into February. How about khaki?
    - ❏ 1 dressy. Choose a seasonless fabric and three-quarter length sleeves, and you'll have something versatile enough to wear this early in September and into those colder months.

- ❏ Pants
    - ❏ 1 pair of jeans
    - ❏ 2 pairs of corduroys or gabardines. If you make one pair black, you can dress them up for an evening in December with a black sweater.
    - ❏ 1 pair of wool or gabardine, trouser-leg, dressy slacks.

- ❏ Tops
    - ❏ 3 sweaters
    - ❏ 4 shirts or pullovers (one dressy, to wear for the upcoming holidays)

- ❏ Miscellaneous
    - ❏ 1 sweatsuit.

If You Are Due in March or April
You will outgrow your waistband by October–November.
You'll need (weight of fabric depending on the climate):

- ❏ Dresses
    - ❏ 2 casual. The selection in maternity dresses is often bigger and better than separates, and because you can

afford to concentrate on winter, look for two dresses that can get you through a day at work or at home and right on into a casual evening.
- ❏ 1 dressy (to wear for the upcoming holidays)

❏ Pants
- ❏ 1 pair of jeans
- ❏ 2 pairs of winter-weight (corduroy and a stretch velvet make a versatile combo)
- ❏ 1 pair of good wool or gabardine slacks

❏ Tops
- ❏ 3 sweaters (They may take a beating in terms of stretching and tugging.)
- ❏ 4 long-sleeved tops (Blouses, knits, winter pullover, or T-shirt style.)

❏ Miscellaneous
- ❏ A denim jumper in a style that suits your shape best (some have bigger armholes than others) might come in handy throughout your term.

If You Are Due in May or June

You will outgrow your waistband by December–January. You'll need:

❏ Dresses
- ❏ 1 casual. Think spring, even though you may be shopping in February or March. You'll want this casual number to take you into June, if possible.
- ❏ 1 dressy. Make this a simple style so you can wear it for lunch or dinner.
- ❏ 1 sundress. If it is a solid color, you may be able to wear it with a shirt in the cooler months and then all by itself when the weather changes in June.

- ❏ Pants
    - ❏ 1 pair of jeans
    - ❏ 1 pair of corduroys. Pick a pale color so it won't seem out of place in May. The weight will be right for March, too.
    - ❏ 1 pair of cotton trousers. Make these dark-colored slacks so they will work early in your pregnancy, and then again with a summer top toward the end. For instance, black cotton pants can be sweater-layered early on and then used again with a summer top in May or June.
    - ❏ 1 pair of good shorts. In addition to simple running shorts, you'll want something that won't look out of place when you go for a walk on a sweltering day in June.

- ❏ Tops
    - ❏ 2 sweaters. Think about buying one wool or a wool blend and one cotton for warmer weather.
    - ❏ 3 shirts. If you choose a long-sleeved version when you are buying in March or April, why not get something that can be rolled up for a lighter look? A style that is tight at your wrists won't roll up far enough.
    - ❏ 2 T-shirt tops for early summer and late spring. Buy carefully and you may be able to layer these purchases, for earlier wear.

- ❏ Miscellaneous
    - ❏ 1 jumper

If You Are Due in July or August

You will outgrow your waistband by February–March.

You'll need:

- ❏ Dresses
    - ❏ 1 casual
    - ❏ 1 dressy
    - ❏ 1 sundress

- ❏ Pants
    - ❏ 3 pairs of cotton trousers. You may not need jeans if you can squeeze into your regular jeans until early spring.
    - ❏ 1 pair of shorts

- ❏ Tops
    - ❏ 2 sweaters. Pick a blend and a color that will span the seasons and one that can definitely be worn by itself or with a shirt.
    - ❏ 1 long-sleeved maternity top
    - ❏ 2 summer shirts or T-shirts

- ❏ Miscellaneous
    - ❏ 1 bathing suit

If You Are Due in September or October

You will outgrow your waistband by April–May.

You'll need:

- ❏ Dresses
    - ❏ 1 dressy
    - ❏ 2 sundresses. Make sure that one can be worn as a jumper with a blouse or T-shirt underneath.

- ❏ Pants
    - ❏ 2 pairs of cotton trousers. By choosing a dark color for one, you can help it stretch through three seasons.
    - ❏ 2 pairs of shorts, 1 casual, 1 dressy

- ❏ Tops
  - ❏ 1 summer-to-fall sweater
  - ❏ 3 summer tops chosen with layering in mind
  - ❏ 1 long-sleeved maternity top

- ❏ Miscellaneous
  - ❏ 1 seersucker jumper or jumpsuit
  - ❏ 1 bathing suit

If You Are Due in November or December

You will outgrow your waistband by June–July.

You'll need:

- ❏ Dresses
  - ❏ 1 casual
  - ❏ 1 dressy (The holiday season will arrive when you are at your biggest.)
  - ❏ 1 sundress

- ❏ Pants
  - ❏ 1 pair of jeans
  - ❏ 1 pair of corduroy or lightweight wool or gabardine slacks. Look for something in a light corduroy so you can wear them into early October with a sweater.
  - ❏ 1 pair of cotton trousers

- ❏ Tops
  - ❏ 2 sweaters, one lightweight and one woolly for a winter's day
  - ❏ 2 long-sleeved shirts
  - ❏ 2 short summer tops

- ❏ Miscellaneous
  - ❏ 1 bathing suit

Clothing Questions and Answers

What size should you buy? Most women wear their regular size in dresses and tops. However, if you are busty, you may want to go up. Because most maternity clothes are cut larger and looser, you can probably check adjacent sizes for all your needs. One size smaller or larger doesn't make any difference. In slacks or skirts, you will probably be one or two sizes larger than your normal number. Most women gain weight in their thighs, and this is where you need that extra room. Though some manufacturers claim that women should always buy their regular size, this isn't always true. Aim for the rack near your old size and be creative.

Why should you spend money on clothes that will fit you for only six months? Because you have fewer choices in your closet, you'll probably be wearing these maternity items much more frequently than your non-maternity clothes. You will get your money's worth. Maternity clothes are worn three times more often during a busy seven-month period of your life, and many women rely on them after the baby arrives, too. With so much else happening to throw you off balance emotionally, it will make you feel better about yourself if you make the effort to look good as your body changes.

How can you tell if the dress you try on in the first trimester is actually going to fit seven months later? Check to see if the shoulder seams are in their proper places. Then, grab some of the fabric right at your bust line to see if it will give another inch or two. If it will, the stomach area will undoubtedly stretch as well.

Why can't you wear large-size regular clothes? You can. Sometimes, this tactic works just perfectly. Be careful about hemlines, however. The front of the dress, for instance, will sneak up and the back will dip down later in pregnancy. Sometimes an outfit is worth buying if you think it can be altered or you know you will wear it for part of your pregnancy and then again after the baby comes.

Will I need special tops if I am going to breast-feed my baby? Not necessarily. Some of your maternity tops are definitely going to have to merge with your postpartum wardrobe. Keep in mind that unbuttoning a blouse with one hand while cradling a baby with the other makes it pretty impossible to appear modest at the same time. Though some experts suggest button-front shirts for breast-feeding moms, soft turtlenecks and loose-fitting T-shirts that can be pulled up may be more useful. Buttoned shirts are best when you need to see exactly what you are doing, if you are in bed nursing your baby, or if you aren't skilled in hooking or unhooking the nursing bra. Pull-up tops are certainly more private, however.

RECORD SHEET:
To Our Baby—A Message from Month Two

PHOTO CAPTION: This picture was taken on_____. It shows

_____.

   Dear Baby:

   Right now, tucked safe and sound in my womb, I'm sure the outside world is something of a mystery to you. Someday, though, I know you'll want to hear all about this special time. That's why I'm recording my thoughts, feelings, and experiences here. I look forward to the future, when we'll have a good time sharing these memories with each other.

   Thoughts and feelings about, and messages to, baby this month:

_____

_____

_____

_____

Important Reminders	Scheduled Activities "To Do"

Now is the time to . . .

- Schedule/confirm your next check-up with your ob/gyn. If your pregnancy is proceeding in a typical fashion, you should be seeing your doctor at least once a month until the seventh month, and more frequently thereafter. Record your next regularly scheduled checkup on the appropriate date in this planner!
- Go to the appointment prepared. Continue to track your symptoms. Draft a list of any questions you have. Bring both lists to your next doctor's appointment.
- Schedule regular beauty treatments, such as a haircut, manicure, and pedicure.
- Schedule and plan regular "date nights" with the father-to-be, at least once a week.
- Consider scheduling a last vacation for just the two of you, somewhere romantic, but nearby.

9 Jan 15 ~~missed period~~

DAY 1

18 Jan 16

DAY 2

17

DAY 3

Scheduled Activities "To Do"	Important Reminders

DAY 4

18

DAY 5

19

DAY 6

20

Now is the time to . . .

Avoid second-hand smoke. Even though you may not be lighting up yourself, you are a passive smoker when you are with anyone else, including your husband, and unavoidably inhaling the stream from a lit cigarette. Smoking, as well as ambient or second-hand smoke, leads you to create excess carbon monoxide, which combines with hemoglobin and takes oxygen from your fetus. Smoke can lead to ear, nose, and throat infections later, as well as bronchitis, asthma, and respiratory problems. A condition known as placental abruption, in which the placenta actually detaches from the side of the uterus, is also related to tobacco abuse. Your risk of miscarriage increases. Ask people, including your mate, friends, and relatives, to step outside if they insist on smoking.

Did you know that . . .
The nicotine in cigarettes slows up in the blood flow to the placenta, which is keeping your baby alive inside you?

Important Reminders	Scheduled Activities "To Do"

Now is the time to . . .

Avoid alcohol. Alcohol consumption during the first trimester is particularly troublesome. Niels Lauerson, M.D., a New York obstetrician and gynecologist, has stated, "In the first three months of pregnancy, when biological systems—especially the nervous system—are forming and the fetus is most vulnerable, alcohol can have a particularly damaging effect." Dr. Lauerson was discussing women who were drunk on a consistent or daily basis when he made the above comment. Unfortunately, reports Lauerson, "The FDA is unable to set a 'safe' level for alcoholic consumption during pregnancy."

Some doctors, such as Dr. Howard Berk, believe that two to four drinks a week will not produce fetal alcohol syndrome. Lauerson believes that if you do feel the need to have a social drink, the second and third trimesters are a less worrisome time to indulge. Even then, it's important to watch your intake of vital nutrients. Alcohol, Lauerson explains, absorbs your body's nutrients, so "make sure you increase your intake of essential nutrients and vitamins."

Even better, why not just let the urge to drink pass altogether—and look forward to that first beer or glass of wine as a just reward after your baby is safely delivered and, if you plant to breastfeed, breastfeeding is over?

21

DAY 7

22

DAY 8

23

DAY 9

Scheduled Activities "To Do"	Important Reminders

DAY 10

24

DAY 11

25

DAY 12

26

Now is the time to . . .

Schedule a dental appointment.
As the fetus gets bigger, it can
drain important nutrients, such as
calcium, from the mother. In
addition, your gums may bleed
because the tissues of your mouth
have become softer. For these
reasons, it's important to touch
base with your dentist. Schedule a
thorough cleaning for your teeth
right away. Schedule additional
visits at your dentist's
recommendation. Be extra
vigorous about brushing and
flossing. Ask your physician about
calcium supplementation. Make
sure you eat adequate amounts of
dairy products.

Important Reminders	Scheduled Activities "To Do"

Now is the time to . . .

Enjoy some peace and quiet.
Everyone needs a quiet hour, half-hour, or even ten minutes of serenity a day. Highly successful people claim that it sharpens their minds and relaxes their bodies. When you are pregnant, you especially need to sit quietly and daydream a little each day. If utter stillness makes you antsy to get up and move, try browsing in a bookstore, walking around the block, or pursuing any kind of mindless, yet pleasurable, activity.

Did you know that . . .
• Napping can help you think straight for up to ten hours after you wake up?
• Not drinking enough water can make you feel sleepy?

27

28

29

DAY 13

DAY 14

DAY 15

Scheduled Activities "To Do"	Important Reminders

DAY 16

30

DAY 17

31

DAY 18

32 Feb 1

Now is the time to . . .

Go shopping for some "comfort foods." Stock up on the following food items, which have a fairly long shelf life, and which many pregnant women say have helped ease them through morning sickness:

- Crackers
- Toast
- Fruit
- Fruit sorbets
- Ice cream
- Yogurt
- Dry cereal
- Bread sticks
- Rice cakes
- Plain popcorn
- Potatoes (to bake)

Did you know that . . .
Morning sickness makes 50 percent of all women nauseous?

Still feeling a bit under the weather? F.Y.I, during the second month, it's perfectly normal to continue to experience typical symptoms of pregnancy, such as . . .

- Tender breasts
- Fatigue
- Occasional dizziness
- Frequent urination
- Nausea
- Insomnia
- Constipation
- Indigestion
- Stomach as well as intestinal gas
- Runny nose
- Headaches
- Vaginal discharge
- Cravings for strange foods
- Aversions to old favorites
- Changes in skin and hair

2

DAY 19

3

DAY 20

4

DAY 21

Scheduled Activities "To Do"	Important Reminders

DAY 22

5

DAY 23

6

DAY 24

7

Now is the time to . . .

Chill out! Kick back! In other words, continue cutting back on unneccessary commitments.

- Start by listing your priorities for the month ahead, and don't expect to accomplish anything other than the top items on your list!
- Lower your goals. Ask yourself, what can you live without? How can you streamline your household and work responsibilities?
- Don't be such a perfectionist when it comes to work, socializing, volunteer activities, or household chores. Schedule a break into each and every day.
- Consider hiring a cleaning person to help out around the house, especially during the last few months of the pregnancy and during the first few months after baby's birth. Start planning now for ways to manage the challenging months ahead.

Important Reminders	Scheduled Activities "To Do"

Now is the time to . . .

Start shopping for some comfortable clothing. Even though you probably haven't outgrown the waistlines on your skirts, slacks, and dresses yet, maternity clothes are beckoning. What will you need? Where will you shop? Start the process slowly. First on the list is a comfortable bra that will support your increasingly large breasts. Next, consider

- essentials, such as
- underwear
- night clothes
- T-shirts
- exercise wear
- a pair of black leggings for pulling on beneath big shirts and sweaters

Some women are truly gifted at getting by with less. Others absolutely need more variation and changes in order to feel happy and comfortable. With today's assortment of stretch fabrics that actually let your skin breathe too, you may be able to get by far longer with your own clothes, completely avoiding the maternity clothes issue or at least delaying it until that last trimester. Or, you could start borrowing basics from your husband's side of the closet. Man-tailored shirts, suit vests, his baggy sweaters, elastic waist jogging shorts, his large T-shirts, windbreakers, barn jackets, and outerwear can help you stretch your clothing dollars.

DAY 25

DAY 26

DAY 27

Scheduled Activities "To Do"	Important Reminders

DAY 28

11

DAY 29

12

DAY 30/31

13 + 14

Now is the time to . . .

Make plans for announcing your pregnancy.

Some women choose to wait until they are well into their tenth, eleventh, or twelfth week to tell anyone other than the man in their life that they are pregnant. Most miscarriages occur in these first few weeks of pregnancy, so sometimes announcing a pregnancy too soon can make life uncomfortable later if you lose the baby. The burden of carrying such a big secret can be either deliciously pleasant or uncomfortably weighty. Some want to shout the good news from every rooftop immediately. That's fine, too.

Even if you choose to wait to share the good news, you can give some thought now to how you might want to celebrate the announcement, and which close family members and friends you want to share it with.

No matter which approach you choose, now, as the second month ends and the third month begins, is a time of settling into the impact of your new state. Plan to take every opportunity to enjoy it to the fullest extent possible.

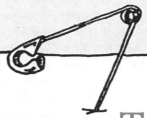

Month Three

Pee-ing into little cups like a pro,
Getting weighed, measured, poked, prodded,
Telling others that, "Yes, it's true. . . ."
Some days, your smile says it all.

TO DO THIS MONTH

- [ ] Tell people your good news.
- [ ] Steal time for yourself (even ten minutes a day!).
- [ ] Talk about tests with your doctor.
- [ ] Don't worry about your weight.
- [ ] Take a good look in your medicine cabinet.
- [ ] Go bra shopping.

You've made it to Month Three of your pregnancy—the month that marks the end of the first trimester, and the month when you may start to settle into the reality of your condition: Peeing into little cups like a pro, getting weighed, measured, poked, and prodded. It's the month when you find yourself telling yourself—and, quite possibly others—that, "Yes, it's true . . ."

Women adapt to pregnancy in different ways, according to Atlanta pediatrician Sandy Matthews, who has watched thousands of expectant moms in her more than thirty-year old practice. "I like to think of living in a pregnant state in the same vein as learning to ride a bicycle," he insists. "When you first got up on that bicycle seat, you felt a little shaky. Maybe you fell off. But, you kept climbing back up to try it again because that new sensation was exhilaratingly different. Finally, then, you started speeding along. It was a unique talent or ability that you had all along."

By now, some of the good habits you've started to establish during the first two months should be becoming second nature to you now. You should continue to:

- ♂ Prioritize your time—putting the priority on stealing time for rest, relaxation, and enjoying private time with your husband.
- ♂ Maintain a schedule of regular beauty treatments and taking every opportunity to pamper yourself.
- ♂ Eat healthfully and exercise moderately.
- ♂ Take doctor prescribed vitamins/supplements.
- ♂ Read about your unborn baby.
- ♂ Record your symptoms.
- ♂ Practice Kegel exercises.

Although it may still feel a bit new to you, try to relax a bit into your pregnancy now. As long as you practice good health practices, stop worrying about your weight. If you haven't already done so, prepare to share the news of your happiness with loved ones and good friends.

❏ Talk about tests with your doctor.
❏ Evaluate your medicine cabinet.
❏ Go bra shopping.
❏ Consider telling people your good news.

Talk about Tests with Your Doctor

The better you get at asking questions, the easier it will be to obtain the information you need to manage your pregnancy.

⚘ Use open-ended questions. Begin with *who, what, when, where*, and *how*. If you use *why* as an opener, you may put your doctor on the defensive.

⚘ Tone of voice is critical. If you are preoccupied, hungry, furious, frustrated, or too tired to think straight, you are not going to be able to ask good questions or hear answers clearly.

⚘ Face the person to whom you are speaking. If you are asking questions when you are up on the examining table and your doctor's head is not even in your line of vision, you are not going to be able to have a proper discussion.

⚘ Get clarification for anything·you don't understand.

⚘ Be specific. What exactly does your doctor mean? Are you being bombarded by medical terms you don't understand? Don't worry about appearing stupid. Take it slow. If a word is unclear, politely ask for an explanation. If the issue of a particular test comes up, ask exactly what he intends to find out from the results of

the procedure. Reserve the right to ask additional questions later, too.

What to Ask Your Doctor

You've probably been to visit your doctor or midwife's office at least twice by now. Perhaps you've settled into a happy routine and look forward to these updates. However,

- ⚥ Are you comfortable with him/her?
- ⚥ Are you getting all your questions answered?
- ⚥ Have you settled any concerns about insurance, payments, managed care plans, and other frustrating paperwork problems?

You may have special concerns and requests. For instance, what is this doctor's cesarean rate? What is her approach to pain medication during labor and delivery? Write down your questions beforehand. Do your homework. Ask other mothers, friends, and relatives for inside tips on making your pregnancy go as smoothly as possible. And, remember, your doctor or midwife is a professional who is working for you. You have hired this individual, and you should never feel belittled or feel childish in his or her presence. You have more power than you think.

Evaluate Your Medicine Cabinet

Your first and last trimesters are the most critical periods of development for your baby. Yet, making expectant mothers anxious about medication has only recently been considered appropriate. According to Dr. Howard Berk, new scientific evidence supports his belief that, "Anything you can buy over the counter, you can take when you are pregnant."

Aspirin was once considered a problem, but unless you are in your last three weeks, it's no longer considered dangerous. Connecticut obstetri-

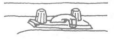

cian-gynecologist and author Howard Shapiro states, "Almost all chemical substances can cross the placenta and become concentrated in the fetus. Whether or not a drug causes harm depends on many factors, including the genetic makeup of the mother and fetus, the specific chemical structure of the drug, the month of pregnancy in which the drug is used, and the total dose." Actually, the placenta is a filter that has the ability to screen out substances above a certain size. Small molecules get through and others don't. That's why if you have the flu, the flu won't affect the baby. Yet, small viruses like herpes and chicken pox can get through. This filtering process protects your baby. If there is a question, consult with your practitioner. In the meantime, don't worry, says Berk. You don't need to live in fear of every move you make or every burp you take.

The Food and Drug Administration (FDA) continues to study the issue of medications during pregnancy. If you are interested in doing your own research about drugs during pregnancy and have access to the Internet, you might want to visit the Web site called MedicineNet, State of the Art Medical Information (http://medicinenet.com).

Good Advice from the FDA

All over-the-counter drugs are required to carry the warning label: "As with any drug, if you are pregnant or nursing, seek the advice of a health professional before using this product." There are five FDA categories of safety, from A (safest) to X (not a good idea at all). Whether you need to take a regular antibiotic, an antiepileptic drug for seizures, or use an asthma inhaler for hay fever season, you should be able to understand the degree of safety. Not all drugs have been assigned one of these lettered categories, and drug manufacturers are not legally bound to publicize FDA pronouncements about a particular medicine. However, these definitions are important to know:

A Controlled studies in women fail to demonstrate a risk to the fetus in the first trimester; there is no evidence of risk in later trimesters, and the possibility of fetal harm appears remote.

B Either animal reproduction studies have not demonstrated a fetal risk, or there are no controlled studies in pregnant women in the first trimester, and there is no evidence of a risk in later trimesters.

C Either studies in animals have revealed adverse effects on the fetus (teratogenic, embryocidal, or other), and there are no controlled studies in women, or studies in women and animals are not available. The drug should be given only if the potential benefit justifies the potential risk to the fetus.

D There is positive evidence of human fetal risk, but the benefits from use in pregnant women may be acceptable despite the risk—for example, if the drug is needed for a life-threatening situation, or for a serious disease for which safer drugs cannot be used or are ineffective.

X Studies in animals or human beings have demonstrated fetal abnormalities, or there is evidence of fetal risk based on human experience or both, and the risk of the use of the drug in pregnant women clearly outweighs any of the benefits. The drug is contraindicated in women who are, or may become, pregnant.

Buying a Bra

You'll need a good bra to support your breasts throughout your pregnancy. Many women do not know how to buy a correctly sized bra. Here's how it's done: Measure your chest under your arm and above your bust. This measurement is the bra size, such as 34 or 36. If you get an odd number, add one. For example, a 35 becomes a 36. Next, measure your bust at the fullest point. If your bust number is 1½ inches larger than your chest figure, you are an A cup. 1½ to 2½ inches larger is a B cup, and 3½ to 4½ inches larger is a D cup. For example, if your chest measures 34 inches and your bust beasures 36 inches, your bra size would be a 34 B.

How Your Baby Grows

In the third month, your uterus begins to grow and stretch. The fetus floats inside this roomy space in his or her warm, watery comfort zone, attached to the umbilical cord. With his graceful, weightless movements, his life-support system, and the perils of his existence, it's no wonder at least one scientist nicknamed him an 'intronaut.'

Because fetal muscles and nerves are working together, your baby starts moving at first tentatively, then more seriously. By month's end, he will be moving vigorously. Well-known expert Dr. Virginia Apgar, M.D., says that the fetus kicks, swims, twists, turns around, pivots, and even somersaults. "He can move his thumb in opposition to his fingers. He can open his mouth, swallow, inhale and exhale, curl his toes, bend his wrist and his waist and make a fist. In fact," she states, "an unborn baby can perform many maneuvers in his watery environment five months before his birth that he will not be able to duplicate again until several months after his birth."

Facial features are becoming more pronounced, more human, and more attractive. He or she takes on the physical features of someone in your own family now. The eyes grow closer together. Eyelids have grown long enough to shut now. (They will stay shut until the last trimester.)

Vocal cords are in place, although the fetus isn't yet able to make sounds. Sucking is now possible. Taste buds and saliva glands develop. Soon, when swallowing is developed, the baby will drink amniotic fluid into a newly formed stomach. The amniotic fluid contains nutrients that help the fetus grow. In fact, drinking helps those tiny kidneys to begin processing, and later, the fetus will urinate. Don't worry. Fetal urine is quite sterile and goes directly back into the amniotic fluid.

A fetus may inhale some of the amniotic fluid, but there is no danger of drowning. Your unborn baby isn't breathing—that won't happen until he sees the light of day, even though breathing motions can be detected. All of the oxygen is being supplied by you via the umbilical cord.

Sex organs are visible. Skin is so thin that it is transparent. You can see the blood vessel network clearly. Your baby looks hairy because of a covering of soft down called *lanugo*. The heart is beating twice as fast as yours. Your unborn baby has earlobes.

At the end of month three, the weight of the fetus is approximately $5/8$ of an ounce, or 18 grams. Her length is about 9 centimeters. The fetus looks quite human. Although the head is still disproportionately large for the size of the two-inch body, little fingernails and toenails are growing now.

What You Can Expect to Experience

Emotional Changes

Bike riding on a bumpy, rut-filled road is no easy task. Neither is being pregnant. "Be careful." "Eat this." "Don't drink that." "Be aware of certain signs." "How could you even consider doing that?!!" By twelve weeks, you have reached a point still fraught with all those annoying first-trimester symptoms and concerns, but, rest assured, there is an end in sight. You are up and riding. It's going to get smoother.

In the meantime, though, there are many issues to deal with, issues that naturally make you feel emotional. Among the feelings that many moms-to-be experience at this stage are:

- Anxiety to tell everyone that yes, you are pregnant
- Feeling that your mate's behavior is annoying or worrisome
- Fear of the unknown
- Mixed feelings about parenthood
- Concern over what you feel to be strange side effects or symptoms of pregnancy

Becoming a mother is a challenge. Even if you've already had a child, becoming a mother for the second time requires some adjustments.

During pregnancy, many couples complicate the transition to parenthood by worrying constantly and evaluating each other. Even during the happiest of pregnancies, fear of the unknown can dominate. You and your partner are bound to have mixed feelings. The elation about the news that you both may have experienced months ago could be clouded with concerns now. Talk about it. Don't fume in silence. Don't brood. Get out. Go on a date away from your home. You both need a little romance even if your stomach is still lurching. The food will be less important than the honest conversation.

Taking Care of Yourself

Getting the Most Out of Monthly Checkups: Tests

Testing seems to be the name of the game in modern pregnancies. Not only is your doctor making sure that the unborn baby is growing normally, but also a variety of other concerns are explored. No test is foolproof, of course, but early warnings of trouble are well worth your discomfort or anxiety. Some tests, such as amniocentesis and *alpha-fetoprotein (AFP)*, may be scheduled early in your second trimester.

Urine Tests

Regular samples of urine taken during office visits will show not only that you are pregnant, but also the levels of sugar, protein, and other substances in your body. Signs of urinary infection can also be detected. Traces of sugar can be a sign of diabetes, and too much protein could mean that your kidneys aren't working properly. Later, protein in your urine is a warning of a rare, but serious complication, called *preeclampsia*, or pregnancy-induced high blood pressure. The most important substance in your urine right now is *human chorionic gonadtropin*, or HCG, which is produced by the embryo as it becomes attached to your uterus. A hormone, HCG streams into your circulation, moves through your kidneys, and is later excreted through your kidneys. In your third trimester, HCG levels dissipate.

A Pap Smear Will Rule Out Cancer

If you've been having regular gynecological checkups, you probably already know that your doctor will scrape your cervix during an internal examination to test cells for signs of cancer. When you are pregnant, pap smear results can be confusing because of the biochemical changes in your body. If the test turns up positive the first time, a second pap smear may be required for another opinion. Relax. Mention your concerns to your doctor. The American College of Obstetricians and Gynecologists now requires all women to have a pap test within three months of pregnancy.

Giving Blood

The amount of blood in your body actually increases when you are pregnant. In fact, the fluid portion goes up by approximately 40 percent. Meanwhile, your red blood cell count may rise by about 20 percent. This disparity—the increase in plasma but not quite as much in red blood cells—can cause anemia. Blood testing will check for anemia, or lack of iron, as well as sexually transmitted diseases. Blood tests also determine whether or not you are immune to German measles or rubella. Even if you can't remember if you had it or not, your blood will tell the truth. German measles or rubella can cause birth defects, especially if you contract the infection during the first trimester. Babies whose mothers contracted rubella early in pregnancy can end up with cataracts (eye problems), heart defects, and deafness. A majority of women have been exposed to the rubella virus or have been vaccinated against it before becoming pregnant, however. Immunity lasts a lifetime. By the end of the first trimester, the risk to your unborn baby is smaller.

Testing also tells the doctor your blood type as well as your rhesus, or Rh, factor. Your blood belongs to one of four major groups: A, B, AB, or O. Your blood is also rhesus (Rh) positive, or rhesus (Rh) negative. The word *rhesus* comes from the rhesus monkeys that were used in the first laboratory experiments with red blood cells. If you are Rh-negative and your unborn baby is positive, you could have complications. Only women who are negative need to be concerned, in fact. If an Rh-negative mom's blood somehow combines with the baby's Rh-positive blood, her immune system may try to fight off the baby as an intruder, causing prenatal death or brain damage in the baby. In essence, mother and baby are incompatible. You'll be screened for signs of these antibodies and given an injection of an anti-Rh immunoglobuin (Rhogam) when you reach the twenty-eighth week of pregnancy. The injections stop your immune system from creating antibodies that could hurt your baby.

Blood tests can also indicate inherited anemia. For example, the sickle cell trait can be determined for African or Indian couples who must be particularly sensitive to this situation. Thalassemia can be a problem for families of Mediterranean, Middle East, or Far East origins.

Blood Pressure

The doctor, midwife, or nurse assistant will be measuring your blood pressure at each visit. To take your blood pressure, your practitioner will use a stethoscope and a device called a *sphygmomanometer* that has an inflatable cuff that wraps around your arm, and a pressure gauge. The reading obtained will consist of two numbers separated by a slash mark. You may hear it referred to as 120 over 70, normal, or 140 over 90, which is high and a reason to worry. The first number, known as *systolic pressure*, is the pressure of your arteries as your heart contracts. The second number, *diastolic pressure*, is being measured when your heart is relaxed in between contractions.

Because you are pregnant, your blood pressure may be a little lower than normal. Meanwhile, a rise in blood pressure can alert the doctor to several problems, including preeclampsia. A slight rise in blood pressure doesn't mean you have developed hypertension or a chronic condition. Just sitting there waiting in the doctor's office, anticipating the fact that you will be weighed, measured, poked, and prodded can make your blood pressure rise. If you are anxious about test results, your concern can also cause a temporary rise. So can exercise, stress, or even normal activity. Make sure you are told what your blood pressure is. It's always on your chart, so if you have forgotten to ask, take a look.

Getting Weighed

Getting weighed is routine fare for these regular pregnancy checkups. Be prepared to see the numbers go up consistently. Don't make yourself depressed or crazy about your gain, however. Keep your focus on a healthy baby and a healthy pregnancy, not on some preconceived chart of perfect pounds gained and lost.

Having an Ultrasound

Your practitioner may choose to order an *ultrasound* to get a closer look at the progress inside your uterus. The picture, or *sonogram*, is obtained when high-frequency sound waves, which you can't hear, are passed over your growing uterus with a little hand-held machine called a *transducer*. These waves penetrate your body, send back a living, moving image of the tiny being inside, and transmit the picture to a computer or television screen. You can "see" the baby weeks before the heartbeat can even be heard or detected. Ultrasounds do not rely on radiation, and absolutely no side effects have ever been found. Both kids and moms are safe. Don't forget to ask for a copy of the picture. This marvelous piece of technology is now available in hospitals, clinics, and testing centers, as well as doctor's offices.

The ultrasound is also used for diagnostic tests that can be performed as early as five weeks and will allow you to rest assured about a variety of factors: Is your baby growing steadily? Is he breathing? Is she moving? In fact, are you carrying a boy, a girl, or twins? How is your placenta positioned? What's the heart rate? Is there enough amniotic fluid? Certain birth defects can also be determined early in pregnancy. Placental abnormalities, an ectopic pregnancy, or other abnormalities of pregnancy can show up on an ultrasound. If you are experiencing any kind of unusual bleeding, an ultrasound is the best tool for aiding the doctor in a diagnosis.

If you are scheduled for an ultrasound early in pregnancy before Week 20, for instance, the doctor may ask you to drink plenty of water before you arrive. Sound waves or beams actually need fluid for better conduction. That can translate into three or four glasses up to an hour before appointment time without freedom to go to the bathroom. (Your bladder control will get a workout on ultrasound days!) A full bladder helps the technician create the perfect picture of your uterus. The pelvic organs are easier to see, too, because the bladder actually pushes your bowel up and out of the way. Later in pregnancy, drinking up to the breaking point may not be necessary before an ultrasound because the enlarged uterus sits right on top of your pubic bone and amniotic fluid helps the process go smoother.

Be forewarned that there are two types of ultrasound scans: the *transabdominal*, or across the abdomen, and the *transvaginal*, or directly into your vagina. In very early pregnancy, the technician may opt for the vaginal approach, which means that the transducer will be inserted into your vagina. Be sure to ask which one you will be having so you aren't surprised. Abdominal ultrasounds are the most common.

You will climb up on the table and be asked to pull up your shirt or hospital gown to expose the lower part of your abdomen, from the bottom of your rib cage to your pelvis. Then, a thin application of paste, jelly, or oil will be spread over the skin on your abdomen to improve the contact between the transducer and the machine recording the sound waves. The technician will pass the transducer back and forth across your abdomen, sending and receiving the waves that help create the image you'll see on the screen. Don't let your husband miss this appointment. The chance to see your developing baby moving, sucking a thumb, kicking, turning, twisting inside your womb can be a life-changing experience.

An ultrasound test costs anywhere from $200 to $500, but it's not possible to schedule one on your own. Talk to your doctor about reasons to order the test.

The CVS Test

CVS stands for *chorionic villus sampling*. This is a test that can be done during the first trimester if your doctor is worried about chromosome or biochemical abnormalities in the unborn baby. An ultrasound will be used to guide a soft tube to the tiny chorionic villi, which surround the embryo. Then, a sample, or biopsy, of the chorion is obtained, and the cells are tested. CVS can be performed several weeks before amniocentesis, a test that is not considered accurate until you are nearly into your second trimester. Amniocentesis testing results can take up to ten days to obtain while CVS conclusions are drawn quicker. The CVS cytologist, or cell specialist, does not need to prepare a culture but can examine the fresh cells right away. Some answers can be obtained within forty-eight hours after a CVS. An early diagnosis of Down's syndrome, for instance, may be important for some couples to know. If there is a history of genetic defects in your family, this may also be a very good reason to go for the CVS. Note:

⚥ If you are being offered the option of a CVS, there are several issues of safety and procedure you should be sure to bring up with your doctor. The chance of miscarriage from CVS is up to 30 percent, according to some experts. If your pregnancy is a hard-won state of being, and you spent months, or even years, reaching this point in your first trimester, you may not want to risk losing your baby now. Speak up and have your doctor research the very latest statistics as well as methods. Keep in mind these factors, too:

⚥ CVS is not always accurate. The exact spot where the technician removes the cell sampling from the chorion can be critical. In some cases, cells have been inaccurately taken from the mother's own tissue, which would offer no indication of the health of the unborn baby. Also, some abnormalities in chorionic tissues do not always show up in the fetus. Ask for clarification or a second opinion of any negative CVS report before you decide on any course of action in your pregnancy.

✂ Find out which CVS method will be used on you. CVS relies on an ultrasound machine to guide the tube inside you, but the catheter can be inserted either through your vagina (transvaginally) or directly down through your abdomen (transabdominally). If your doctor has not discussed the difference between the two, don't schedule the test until you get a full report. Published research doesn't show any real differences between the two, so pick your physician's brain about his preferences.

Checking Your Legs, Ankles, and Hands for Swelling

When you are up on the examining table during a regular pre-natal check-up, you should not be surprised to see the doctor or midwife gently poke the skin on your lower legs, your ankles, and your hands. In pregnancy lots of women develop fluid buildup, but excessive swelling could mean the development of high blood pressure or preeclampsia.

Prodding the Abdomen

An old-fashioned, but remarkably accurate, clue to how your pregnancy is progressing is to have your doctor or nurse-midwife gently feel for the top of your womb. A tape measure is also an option because your uterus grows at a steady rate, two or three centimeters per month, until it pushes up above your belly button (at twenty weeks) and reaches just below your rib cage.

Managing Your Weight

Pregnancy is really a high cholesterol state brought on by your hormones. Some doctors feel that an excess weight gain during these nine months can be the start of arteriosclerotic problems. That's why you really need to define what you mean by excess weight. Four to five pounds a month is not an excessive amount to gain, but twelve pounds can be. If you were left alone without any advice and you ate a well-balanced, constant diet, you would gain one-half of your weight in the first six months, and the second half in the last three months. A pregnant patient with excess weight gain in the first and second trimester can double her weight in the last trimester. Someone who has gained ten pounds a month may begin to gain twenty pounds a month. All pregnant women say they are going to lose weight in the postpartum period, but it is the most difficult thing to do right after birth. What most women should aim for is a gain of twenty to twenty-five pounds, an amount that can be lost at delivery. You really don't have to sacrifice your vanity to have a baby. Write down your diet for one week to keep track of excess calories and remain conscious of what you eat.

Managing Emotional Stress

Have you been preoccupied with strange, unexplainable side effects? Get the answers to all your questions. Don't ever fall for the line that you are reading or worrying too much for your own good. Those days of keeping patients in the dark are gone. Are you worried about the health of your baby? Are you frightened that the testing your practitioner has scheduled for the coming weeks may cause a miscarriage? Speak up, and if you don't get the answer you need, consider switching to an expert who will be more forthcoming. Remember: you are not crazy. You are not paranoid. You are not anything but pregnant.

Should You Be Worried about Being Worried?

While it's only natural to feel a certain amount of anxiety about all the unknowns of pregnancy, perhaps you sense that your level of unhealthy stress seems to be escalating week-by-week and worry that it will affect your unborn baby. Researchers have never uncovered any evidence that emotional ups and downs adversely affect a healthy pregnancy. The effects of severe stress, however, are quite different.

How can you define high stress? You are the best person to determine what sends you off the top of the stress scale and into unhealthy territory. If you are working outside your home in an environment that offers you little control but features high levels of emotional stress, then you probably know who you are. Look for ways to eliminate anxiety, and you may even lessen your need for pain medication during labor and birth. Yale University experts discovered that if you exhibit high anxiety during pregnancy, you fall into the category of women who need the most medication.

If you are working or living under chronically stressful conditions, give yourself permission to seek support, advice, and professional counsel from your obstetrician. You're not being a wimp at all. You are actually protecting the life of your unborn baby. In 1990, a University of North Carolina study found that high levels of stress led to low-birth-weight babies and complications during pregnancy, such as hypertension, preeclampsia, and premature birth.

Here are tips to put back some measure of control of your biology and your growing baby:

- Simply recognizing the connection between stress and your health is a step in the right direction.

   Researchers at Penn State found that women who pushed themselves to the limits, working till the end of their pregnancies in what they called "stand up" jobs, were more likely to have placental problems, including areas of dead tissue in the placenta caused by impaired blood flow. Although babies did not show long-term mental or physical impairment, slowing down to a more leisurely pace turned out to be as important mentally as it was physically.

- If you can't come up with concrete ways to escape your stressful situation, experts like Dr. Moskowitz believe that your coping style can make a world of difference. Take a long look at your

approach to this pregnancy. Which one of these personality types fits you best?

- *You create loving bonds.* You have a sense of humor. You anticipate conflicts and how they will make you feel. You consciously put off stresses you know you aren't ready to handle. You know how to turn your own socially unacceptable behavior into something useful. For example, an overeater might "harness her basic eating drive into a career as a gourmet chef." Turn anxiety and curiosity about the entire pregnancy process into a very personal research project.
- *You alienate people.* You deny needing help and don't take responsibility for your actions. You tend to block out your emotions, often unconsciously. You are impulsive in destructive ways. Self-righteous, you project feelings onto others that aren't there. Perhaps you are accusing your husband of not caring enough about the pregnancy or not planning far enough ahead for the birth. You turn minor aches into major diseases or baby disasters.

"The differences between these two coping styles is astounding," according to Dr. Moskowitz. See where you fit in and work to change the way you handle stress.

Preparing for an Emergency

Most pregnancies have happy endings. Yet, you might feel that everything about your pregnancy can be a cause for worry on occasion. Your body may not feel familiar, so why shouldn't creepy symptoms keep you up at night? If you've been placed into a high-risk category because of a combination of factors, then even the simplest, yet unusual, symptoms can be frightening. Never hesitate to call your doctor or midwife about anything. No question is too silly to ask. No sensation is too mild to mention.

According to a study conducted by psychologist Erling Anderson of the University of Iowa, heart surgery patients who have prepared for surgery by becoming more knowledgeable about the procedure report less fear and have an easier recovery period. Pregnancy and childbirth are no different. "Information per se is not inherently reassuring," Dr. Anderson stated. "But it is necessary because people can use it to plan ways to deal with what's happening."

Here are just some of the factors that may have placed you into a high-risk situation and will make your case even more important for your practitioner to watch closely.

Emergencies can happen any time during a pregnancy, but knowing that you are in a high-risk situation is important for both you and your physician to take into consideration. Go over this list of potential reasons for considering your pregnancy high risk. These are certainly issues you have already discussed with your medical team, but just in case, make a note of any that fit your situation.

When to call your doctor

If you experience any of the following signs, contact your practitioner right away. Don't panic. Everything might be perfectly fine, but don't hesitate to make the call.

- Vaginal bleeding
- Abdominal cramping
- A severe headache
- Leaking something watery (amniotic fluid?)
- Painful and frequent urination
- Swollen joints, hands, or face
- Vomiting and nausea that is extreme, constant, and more than any morning sickness you may have experienced
- Dizziness or fainting
- A temperature higher than 101 degrees Fahrenheit

Personal Medical History Worksheet

1. Is there a history of diabetes in your family? In fact, do you have diabetes?

   _____

2. High blood pressure?

   _____

3. Heart problems?

   _____

4. Tuberculosis?

   _____

5. Asthma and/or allergies?

   _____

6. Thyroid disorder?

   _____

7. Any uterine or pelvic abnormalities? Fibroid tumors? Ovarian cysts?

   _____

8. Have you been diagnosed with a sexually transmitted disease?

   _____

9. Does your family's genetic history place you in a high-risk category, too?

   _____

10. Your age is a factor and you are considered high risk. Are you a teenager or over thirty-five?

    _____

11. Did you experience a problem giving birth or during a previous pregnancy? A miscarriage? Stillbirth? Premature birth? Cesarean section?

    _____

What about the Possibility of Miscarriage?

It's not unusual to be concerned about the possibility of miscarriage. Vaginal bleeding is often the first sign of an impending miscarriage, so you have every reason to worry if you notice spots of blood on your underpants. Yes, of course, those stains can be enough to make your heart drop straight through the floor. Yet, staining does not always indicate the beginning of the end of your pregnancy, and more than 20 percent of women who bleed early in pregnancy go on to deliver healthy babies. Sometimes, if the spotting occurs very early in those first days of pregnancy, the blood is just a sign of implantation, indicating that the fertilized egg is attaching itself to the lining of your uterus. If you have had sex with your mate, a bit of blood can be caused by the contact during intercourse.

Bleeding, in fact, is not dangerous when it comes from your cervix. If the bleeding is from your uterus, it is more serious. Your doctor may even ask if it is bright red blood or darker in color. A dark blood stain is a sign of bleeding that occurred several days before. If your bleeding is bright red and you also have low back pain and abdominal cramping, call your doctor immediately.

If you have children already, you are more likely to experience some bleeding. However, bleeding a bit during the same time of the month that you would have expected to be getting your period is not normal during pregnancy. If you notice blood, call your doctor, lie down (preferably on your left side), and try not to panic. Bleeding can start and stop on its own. If the bleeding is slight and stops on its own, your chances of delivering a healthy baby are fine. More than one instance of bleeding or prolonged bleeding during the first trimester should put you and your doctor on edge, however. Statistics on miscarriage differ, but the American College of Obstetricians and Gynecologists (ACOG) reports that 15 to 20 percent of all pregnancies end in miscarriage in the first thirteen weeks. Your risk of miscarriage decreases dramatically after the first trimester, and after hearing your baby's heartbeat, that risk drops even further to about 3 percent.

If Someone Uses the Expression . . .

Threatened miscarriage. Your bleeding is light. You may even spot on and off for several days. Your cervix remains closed. You don't have great pain and losing your baby is not inevitable. Ultrasound will determine what's actually happening and a blood test will check the levels of HCG, the pregnancy hormone. A physical examination will not alter the circumstances one way or the other, but you will want to have a doctor's medical opinion and recommendations.

Inevitable miscarriage. Your bleeding continues steadily. You have started to experience contractions. You may have low back pain or abdominal cramps. Your physician has discovered that your cervix is dilated. In this situation, a miscarriage is inevitable and will probably occur within twenty-four hours. If you notice that you are passing clots of blood, mixed with other fluids and you are in pain, you are in the midst of what is sometimes called a *spontaneous abortion*. In a complete and spontaneous miscarriage, all the placental and fetal tissue is expelled from your uterus. Sometimes a doctor may ask you to save the fetus and placenta in a clean container so it can be examined later. This may be simply impossible or emotionally tricky. However, keep in mind that your doctor is not trying to put you up to some horribly cruel task. His or her goal is to uncover what went wrong so it won't happen again. If your miscarriage is complete, your pain, as well as the bleeding, will stop and you'll be physically fine in a few days. Your uterus will even contract back to its prepregnant size.

Incomplete abortion. Your body has expelled most of the placenta and fetus but not all. If parts remain in the uterus, you could experience heavy bleeding and your uterus will not be able to contract to stop the flow. Hemorrhaging is a possibility. A procedure called a *dilatation and curettage*, known simply as a "D & C" will be on your doctor's list of orders. During a D & C, your cervix is widened, and the remaining tissue is scraped or suctioned out.

Missed abortion. Occasionally, the fetus dies even earlier, in the first eight weeks of development, but remains in your womb. You don't experience any bleeding or pain, but you start to suspect something is not quite right. For instance, your breasts may not be quite as tender as they were earlier in your pregnancy, or morning sickness could have disappeared. What's happened is that levels of HCG have dropped even though the fetus and placenta remain in your uterus. An ultrasound can confirm this, and you will definitely be scheduled for a D & C. The diagnosis of a missed abortion used to be more common, but nowadays, close monitoring during this first trimester makes it less likely to miss for very long. Keep a record of your symptoms, and if you suddenly "don't feel pregnant anymore," tell your doctor right away. Don't wait until your next appointment.

Why Do Miscarriages Occur?

About half the time, miscarriages are caused by chromosomal abnormalities in the fetus, or what's known as a blighted ovum. A random mistake of nature, a blighted ovum is not something you need to worry about in your future pregnancies.

Other factors to be considered in a miscarriage are:

- Hormonal deficiencies
- Anatomical problems in your cervix or uterus
- Incompatible blood types or the Rh factor
- Viruses and infections
- Immune disorders

The wave of emotions following a miscarriage run the gamut from grief, guilt, fear, anger, blame, frustration, and a real sense of personal failure. Others may not understand your feelings because your pregnancy may have been a very private affair up until this point. Yet, even though you may have been pregnant for only a few weeks, don't take this brief state of affairs lightly. Your dreams may have been dashed. The picture you created in your mind's eye of a happy baby was quite real—and so is your loss. Trying to pretend that it was no big deal is not the answer. Don't play the "If only" game, either, thinking of endless "If only I hadn't carried . . . had sex . . . exercised that morning . . . stayed up late . . . skipped my vitamins . . . " Every woman is different, and even a sense of relief can make you feel embarrassed or upset. You have a right to your emotions, and, following a miscarriage, you can expect those emotions to swing wildly. Ask your doctor or someone at the hospital where you were going to deliver to recommend a counseling center or a group where you can share your grief.

Repeated miscarriage? It's important to speak with your doctor, who may want to schedule testing for genetic factors. Scar tissue, endometriosis, cysts, fibroid tumors, or damaged fallopian tubes can also be involved in miscarriages.

When Can I Get Pregnant Again?

Some doctors recommend that you wait at least three menstrual cycles before trying to become pregnant after a miscarriage. Others say it is quite safe to try right away. Every woman is different, and so are you. Don't go on hearsay. Go ahead and speak with your own practitioner, especially if you feel up to trying again right away.

Doctor's Note: Unwarranted Fear of Miscarriage

In pregnancy, some women can have all of the signs of miscarriage, including bleeding and cramps, and not be in danger of losing the baby. This is called *menstrual molimena*, and these symptoms do not represent a threatened miscarriage. What you do is follow the levels of HCG and watch them rise normally. I've had patients who bled through nine months of pregnancy. Their fears ended when they held their beautiful babies.

Baby Gift List

Name	Description of Gift	Thank-you Note Sent (Date)

RECORD SHEET:
To Our Baby—A Message from Month Three

PHOTO CAPTION: *This picture was taken on_____. It shows*

_____.

Dear Baby:
This month has been quite an experience for Mom and Dad.
Here's what we did . . . thought . . . felt . . . and planned:

_____
_____
_____
_____
_____
_____
_____
_____
_____
_____
_____

Important Reminders	Scheduled Activities "To Do"

Now is the time to . . .

- Learn about tests and verify their schedules.

   Testing seems to be the name of the game in modern pregnancies. Not only is your doctor making sure that the unborn baby is growing normally, but also a variety of other concerns are explored. No test is foolproof, of course, but early warnings of trouble are well worth your discomfort or anxiety. Some tests, such as amniocentesis and the alpha-fetoprotein (AFP), may be scheduled early in your second trimester.

   Other tests you may be subject to are:

- Blood tests
- Sonograms
- Pap smears
- *Chorionic villus* sampling

- Schedule/confirm your monthly check-up with your ob/gyn. Record your next regularly scheduled check-up on the appropriate date in this planner!

DAY 1

DAY 2

DAY 3

101

Scheduled Activities "To Do"	Important Reminders

DAY 4

....
....
....
....
....
....
....
....
....
....

DAY 5

....
....
....
....
....
....
....
....
....
....
....
....

DAY 6

....
....
....
....
....
....
....
....
....
....
....
....

Now is the time to . . .

Eliminate the following harmful substances from your medicine cabinet.

- Androgens (used to treat endometriosis)
- Anticoagulants (used to prevent blood clotting)
- Antithyroids (for people with overactive thyroids)
- Anticonvulsants (for seizure disorders or irregular heartbeats)
- Aspirin, or any tablet containing salicylate (for pain relief), during the last three weeks because of bleeding complications, not because it will cause any congenital malformations.
- Chemotherapeutic drugs (used to treat cancer and skin diseases)
- Diethylstilbestrol (once used to treat premature labor and miscarriage; still prescribed for menstrual problems, symptoms of menopause, and breast cancer)
- Isotretinoin (also known as Accutane, prescribed for cystic acne)
- Lithium (used for treatment of depression)
- Streptomycin (antibiotic used for tuberculosis)
- Tetracycline (antibiotic used for a wide variety of infections)

Important Reminders	Scheduled Activities "To Do"

Now is the time to . . .

Forge relationships with medical staff.

Make your relationships with your doctor's staff personal, and you will gain more from the encounters. In fact, the doctor's secretary or office manager may be key to helping you through a myriad of obstacles. Also, think about the nurses and administrative staff in the doctor's office you have met by now. Which ones are your favorites? Do you know their names? Introduce yourself the next time you see them, and take a minute to jot down the name so you can have it for the next visit or the next time you call and end up speaking with someone on the phone other than your doctor.

DAY 7

DAY 8

DAY 9

	Scheduled Activities "To Do"	Important Reminders

Now is the time to . . .

Schedule a sonogram.

   After twenty years of use, ultrasounds are still not always considered routine in the United States, even though they have become absolutely everyday adventures in pregnancy. A sonogram can:

- Check on the health of the fetus
- Determine whether you are carrying a boy or a girl
- Verfy the age of the fetus and the due date

   Experts say that if the ultrasound is done at 16 weeks and beyond, the results are pretty accurate. When an ultrasound is scheduled during the first 12 weeks of your pregnancy, however, the accuracy drops a bit.
   Nevertheless, if you think you would be more comfortable knowing everything is safe and your baby is behaving normally on an ultrasound, simply explain your anxiety to your doctor. Your fears could be reason enough to order the test.

Did you know that . . .
When dating the length of a pregnancy, the ultrasound technician can be accurate within a few days. Ultrasounds also date your pregnancy from the point of conception, which is a few days different from the point of your last period.

DAY 10

DAY 11

DAY 12

Important Reminders	Scheduled Activities "To Do"

Now is the time to . . .

- **Investigate prenatal exercise classes in your area.** If you are uncertain where to begin, ask the experts in your doctor's or midwife's office. Pick up flyers, booklets, or handouts about local classes being held in hospitals, private studios, or sports clubs. Not only will you be taking good care of your body, but also you may be able to network and commiserate with other pregnant women.
- **Take stock of your daily diet.** Are you eating five servings of fruits and vegetables every day? Are you taking your vitamins? Folic acid is absolutely essential to the health of your unborn baby. If you are constipated, drink more water. If you are still suffering from morning sickness, take heart. Most women's stomachs settle down in the second trimester. You are almost there.

DAY 13

DAY 14

DAY 15

Scheduled Activities "To Do"	Important Reminders
DAY 16	***Now is the time to . . .***
	• Listen for the baby's heartbeat. The heart is beating twice as fast as yours and you may be able to hear it now. A Doppler device, which is a combination of ultrasound and amplifier, can sometimes pick up this wonderful sound as early as 10 or 12 weeks. If you don't hear it just yet, though, don't worry. By the 18th week, you are more likely to catch this intriguing noise— music to your ears.
DAY 17	**Pregnant Perk!** • **Plan to Accomplish Less in a Day.** Professional time managers insist on the need to set priorities to meet daily goals. When you give a little of yourself to everything, you commit a great deal of yourself to nothing. Think back to your most fragmented days. Were you trying to complete an impossibly long list of things to do? A good rule of thumb is: never plan more than half your day.
DAY 18	• **Be kind to yourself.** Stop racing and expecting a completed to-do list at the end of your day. Schedule time for naps. Your lungs, kidneys, and heart are all working harder than ever because of the increased volume of blood circulating in your body.

Important Reminders	Scheduled Activities "To Do"

Now is the time to . . .

Buy New Clothes
The waistband on your slacks, jeans, and skirts may feel snug. Take time to treat yourself to something new to wear that won't tug or make you feel as if you have eaten too much.

Did you know that . . .
Weight gain varies tremendously, especially during this first trimester. If you haven't had morning sickness, making it hard to eat, 2½ pounds growth puts you on target. Many women put on much more than this meager beginning, however, and these pounds are quite legitimate. After all, you are growing a new life.

Tip:
Weigh yourself only on Friday. Most of us binge on Saturday or Sunday. Then you can watch your eating habits the rest of the week to see what happens.

DAY 19

DAY 20

DAY 21

Scheduled Activities "To Do"	Important Reminders

DAY 22

DAY 23

DAY 24

Now is the time to . . .

Check out your growing baby.
You can check this growth on your own starting at the end of the first trimester. Go to the bathroom and empty your bladder completely. Then lie down on a hard, flat surface and put your hand just above your pubic bone. If you think you are at least twelve weeks pregnant, then you should be able to feel the uterus. If you sense that your uterus is growing much faster than is considered normal, your hunch could indicate that you are carrying twins, or at least a very large baby. In the last trimester, your tape measure should stretch out to nearly thirty-six centimeters of growth. However, this height may suddenly drop in the last few weeks as your baby begins his escape down and out into the real world through your pelvis.

Important Reminders	Scheduled Activities "To Do"

Now is the time to . . .

- **Be amazed!** Just think, right now, at this very moment in time, you are carrying an unborn baby that looks quite human. The head of your baby-to-be is still disproportionately large for the size of its frail body—a mere two inches in length, but it has all of the physical details that indicate it's a baby, even infinitesimal little fingernails and toenails are growing now. The nutrients it needs for its amazing growth spurt are contained in the amniotic fluid, which it drinks.

- **Feel the change in your body's shape.** The top of your womb should be stretching up above your pubic bone this month. Put your finger just above your pubic bone. That's where the top of your womb is already. Isn't it amazing how this little being you have yet to meet could be changing your very shape?

DAY 25

DAY 26

DAY 27

109

Scheduled Activities "To Do"	Important Reminders

DAY 28

....
....
....
....
....
....
....
....
....
....
....

DAY 29

....
....
....
....
....
....
....
....
....
....
....
....

DAY 30/31

....
....
....
....
....
....
....
....
....
....
....

Now is the time to . . .

Start sharing the good news.
If you haven't already, now may be the right time to share the good news with close family and friends.

Many couples hold back on telling people they are parents-in-the-making out of concern for potential miscarriage.

Statistics on miscarriage differ, but the American College of Obstetricians and Gynecologists (ACOG) reports that 15 to 20 percent of all pregnancies end in miscarriage in the first 13 weeks. Your risk of miscarriage decreases dramatically after the first trimester, and after hearing your baby's heartbeat, that risk drops even further to about 3 percent.

Part Two

The
Second
Trimester

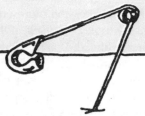

MONTH FOUR

As your stomach settles down, Your energy level goes up, Your jeans refuse to zip, Faint flutterings from deep within take your breath away.

TO DO THIS MONTH

- ❏ Shop for maternity clothes.
- ❏ Get ready to feel your unborn baby move.
- ❏ Go out for dinner.
- ❏ Review amniocentesis with your practitioner.
- ❏ Write down your dreams.
- ❏ Stay cool.
- ❏ Take your vitamins.

During these middle three months of pregnancy, your second trimester, your growing belly becomes more obvious and, yes, getting dressed turns into a new adventure. On the positive side, you are feeling better and more energetic, and every day will become easier. Take a look at yourself in the mirror when you step out of the shower. Go ahead. Don't be afraid. That gentle rounding of your stomach is your baby. Yes, this is the month when, most likely, you'll wake up one morning, put your feet over the side of the bed, and realize, suddenly, the growing impact of the state of pregnancy. The faint flutterings from deep within take your breath away. This will be a busy month. Don't forget to:

- ☿ Shop for maternity clothes.
- ☿ Get ready to feel your unborn baby move.
- ☿ Go out for dinner.
- ☿ Stay cool.
- ☿ Take your vitamins.

This Month's Priorities

Congratulations are in order! At last—you've dreamed of becoming pregnant, and now, you're pretty sure you are. To confirm the good news, you'll want to:

- ❑ Review tests with your practitioner.
- ❑ Schedule test dates.

Review Tests with Your Doctor
Alpha-fetoprotein

Your unborn baby is producing a protein, known as *alpha-fetoprotein (AFP)*, and passing it into your circulatory system. You may be scheduled for a screening blood test, performed by simply drawing blood, to check the level of AFP. Most of the time, a high level of AFP accounts for more than one baby. However, it could mean that your fetus has a neural tube defect. So, if you have a high level, you should have a sonogram to check for the presence of more than one baby. With low AFP, amniocentesis is definitely indicated. The AFP, done between the sixteenth and eighteenth weeks, can also indicate the possibility of Down's syndrome or neural tube defects, which occur once in every 1,000 births. If you have already had a baby with anencephaly or spina bifida, your chances of having another child with a neural tube defect increase significantly. Results of the AFP test are usually available within one week, but the reliability of the outcome is imprecise if your due date hasn't been accurately calculated, if you have diabetes, or you are carrying twins. If the AFP levels are high, the practitioner may recommend a second test or request that you have an ultrasound right away. Rest assured that only a small number of women who have irregular AFP test results actually do give birth to babies with birth defects, according to the American College of Obstetricians and Gynecologists.

An AFP-3 test is a bit more sophisticated than the simple AFP test, and it has proven to pick up signs of Down's syndrome. In what is called a triple screen test, the technician measures your AFP as well as the level of human chorionic gonadotropin (HCG) and estriol, a type of estrogen, in your blood. High HCG and low estriol are signs of possible danger.

Amniocentesis

The water, or amniotic fluid, inside the sac where your unborn baby is growing, can offer experts incredibly detailed information about the developing new life inside you. Amniocentesis is the procedure that makes this screening possible. Under ultrasound guidance, to avoid touching your unborn baby, a needle is inserted into the amniotic sac and amniotic fluid is drawn. Fetal cells are pulled from the fluid and are grown in a laboratory culture for chromosomal analysis. Long before birth, your unborn baby's new life is examined. Not only can the age and sex be determined, but also genetic disorders, metabolic problems, and other kinds of birth defects can be discovered.

Amniocentesis is performed sometime between the fourteenth and eighteenth week of pregnancy. Since you are in your fourth month, this may be an issue you are now facing. Here are reasons why an amniocentesis may be planned during this second trimester:

- Are you over thirty-five? Almost all obstetricians in the United States will recommend that you have one if you are over thirty-five because the risk of carrying a baby with Down's syndrome starts to rise as you get older. However, some doctors believe that using the age of thirty-five is a bit arbitrary. If you are in your thirties and this is your first pregnancy and you are concerned, you may want to schedule the test anyway. When the father is over fifty, amniocentesis could be advised because there may be a connection between paternal age and an increased risk of Down's syndrome.
- Have you had a baby with a genetic disorder? If you've already had a baby with a hereditary or chromosomal abnormality, an amniocentesis could make you feel more comfortable.
- Is their a concern about infection?
- Has your Rh status come up?
- Is there any history of neural tube defects—spina bifida, hemophilia, Tay-Sachs disease, or sickle cell anemia in your family?
- Were your AFP test results worrisome? Even if there is no medical history of concern, if alpha-fetoprotein (AFP), a substance that is produced by the baby in the womb and that passes into your bloodstream, shows up at a higher than normal level, an amniocentesis may help clear up any questions.

How the Amniocentesis Test is Performed

The very idea of someone puncturing your womb with a needle sounds unpleasant. Yet, discomfort may be minimal and the reason for having an amniocentesis could be important. Thousands and thousands of amniocentesis tests are performed routinely without complications. Only 1 in every 100 women experience complications, such as cramps or even a miscarriage. You may even be able to have the test done right there in the doctor's office. At the very most, you'll have to go to the hospital or clinic as an outpatient. Most centers insist on a visit to a genetic counselor who will discuss risks before you sign a consent form. Amniocentesis usually takes only a few minutes, thirty at the most, from beginning to end. Make sure to take your husband or close friend along with you for moral support.

Once you are up on the examining table, the technician will clean the bare skin on your abdomen with an antiseptic solution. The goal of this test is to obtain a vial of your amniotic fluid using a needle that will penetrate right through to the sac that protects your baby. Yes, it may hurt.

Local anesthetic applied to the site at which the needle will be injected can actually feel worse than amniocentesis. Discuss ways of dealing with your discomfort with both your doctor and the technician. Some experts have found that deep relaxation exercises, as well as hypnotism, can make the test go smoother.

One of the reasons for waiting until the fourteenth or fifteenth week is that there is more amniotic fluid present, and the likelihood of sticking the fetus, the placenta, or the umbilical cord with a misplaced needle is low. However, the primary reason to wait until this point in pregnancy is that your fetus will have more cells being sloughed off. Earlier, there may be very few cells present in the amniotic fluid. The results of the test might indicate that everything is fine when, in fact, there weren't enough cells for a true test.

If someone suggests that you have an amniocentesis before the fifteenth week, ask about having a specialist handle the technique. Needle injuries are very rare because the technician's aim is guided by an ultrasound picture every step of the way. Even sudden somersaults or changes in fetal positioning are taken into consideration. Clear amniotic fluid is drawn up and then rapidly sent to the lab for evaluation. The technician will also watch your fetus for a few minutes on the ultrasound screen to make sure everything is fine. Your unborn baby's heart rate is checked. Afterward, you may have a few cramps or a bit of vaginal bleeding. Very slight leaks of amniotic fluid have also been noted. You won't have any restrictions on activity afterward if everything has gone fine.

Yes, There Are Risks . . .

Understanding the possible complications of amniocentesis is important, but try not to dwell on disasters. The American College of Obstetricians and Gynecologists (ACOG) reports only 1 in 200 women will have a miscarriage as a result of amniocentesis. A very small minority have reported trauma to the unborn baby, bleeding in either the placenta or the umbilical cord, inadvertent rupture of the sac, amniotic fluid infections, premature labor, and spontaneous abortion. If you are unlucky enough to experience any aftereffects, call your doctor immediately. You may end up in bed for a few days, but chances are excellent that any leakage or bleeding will stop without further medical intervention. In cases where the needle has actually nicked the baby, doctors can usually see the mark on the skin at birth. Long-term follow-up studies of mothers and babies who have taken advantage of this test show no problems at all.

The worst thing about amniocentesis could be the timing. Because the lab needs up to two weeks to complete the evaluation of the fetal cells in the fluid, you could be forced to face some tough issues at this point in your pregnancy. Why so long for the test results? For a diagnosis, the small sample of fetal cells in the fluid must be grown in a culture. This can take weeks. If you fall into one of those high-risk categories and are waiting to decide whether to proceed with your pregnancy, you could be living on the razor's edge emotionally. By the time the test results are back, you will be halfway through your pregnancy, or close to being twenty weeks pregnant. Not only have you become emotionally attached to this unborn being, but second-trimester terminations are more difficult to perform and have a higher risk of complications.

Prenatal Tests Worksheet

TEST	DATE	RESULTS
AFP		
Amniocentesis		
Ultrasound		
Genetic Testing		
Other		

How Your Baby Grows

Fetal growth is quite dramatic and rapid now. Sleeping and waking, moving, sucking, swallowing, and passing urine, the fetus looks more like a miniature human being every day. While the head has been disproportionately large up until this point, the body is now catching up in size: The length of the fetus stretches from four to eight or ten inches, which could be up to nearly half of what it will be at birth. The weight shoots up from one to six ounces.

Facial features are distinct with eyebrows and eyelashes. Thin, nearly transparent skin is covered with a fine, downy hair known as lanugo. Blood vessels beneath the skin are visible. Thumb-suckers show their penchants to put hand to mouth.

Bones are growing, and signs of the skeleton can be seen. From what are known as *ossification centers* will come the bone cells that fill in and harden. However, this growth process is one that continues long after birth and well into adolescence and young adulthood.

Breathing movements can be seen as the fetus's chest moves in and out. During this fourth month, the heart is pumping blood strong enough and loud enough for you and your doctor to hear.

Fetal blood is being pumped through this little body at about four miles an hour. Instead of going to the developing lungs to obtain fresh oxygen and get rid of carbon dioxide, the fetal blood is pushed out through two large arteries in the umbilical cord and on to the placenta, which looks like a dish, is about three inches in diameter now, and has a unique network of blood vessels. On the way back to the fetus, the blood travels through one large umbilical vein. According to obstetrician and researcher Virginia Apgar, this round trip of fetal blood—through the cord, to the placenta, and back to the tiny little body—takes only about thirty seconds.

The umbilical cord is about as long as the fetus and continues to grow. The average umbilical cord at birth is up to twenty-four inches, but it can be as short as five inches and as long as forty-eight inches. Pressure from the blood being continually pumped through it helps straighten the cord out and keeps it from becoming knotted or getting in the way of your unborn baby's kicks and somersaults. Sex organs are now visible, although ultrasound scans can still miss this bit of information at times.

What You Can Expect to Experience

Emotional Changes

At the Center for the Study of the Psychology of Pregnancy in California, director Nancy L. Robbins, M.S.W, once remarked, "Pregnancy is a great watershed—a profound life transition, after which nothing is ever the same again. During pregnancy, each woman looks deep within herself. It's a time of reevaluation and resolution—reevaluation of how you feel about yourself, your marriage, the relationship with your own parents and how you were raised. It reawakens years of unfinished business. The thoughtful inner work that must go on during this transition to motherhood is vital for each woman as she grows into her new role as mother."

What does all this have to do with your clothes not fitting anymore? A bit. In fact, perhaps more than just a bit. "When things go well," Robbins continued, "this inner turmoil results in feelings of confidence, independence, self-esteem. You come away from the crisis strengthened and adult. You experience the birth as a time of joy." In other words, you are not being frivolous or silly when you take your emotional state seriously. If you find yourself anxious, upset, frustrated, or struggling with a case of the "uglies," then go treat yourself to something beautiful today. Stay one step ahead of the physical changes of pregnancy, if you can, and you'll feel better emotionally.

Out of the mouths of other moms:

"I would get depressed about getting dressed. Yet, I knew it was important for me to stay on an even keel emotionally. I stopped trying to squeeze into the old favorites in my closet and put them out of my sight."

"I was getting up in the morning and trying on ten different outfits before I found one that snapped, buttoned, or didn't fit skintight."

"It's so important to put yourself together neatly when you are pregnant. I know I am spending more time coordinating clothes and thinking about earrings, stockings, matching over-blouses to my regular turtlenecks and reassessing my final look, but it's worth it. My dad recently mentioned that I reminded him of my mother when she was pregnant. 'You look so neat,' he said, and I loved it."

"Even though something might look ridiculous on a hanger, try it on. This is one stage of your life when you can't trust those old clothing instincts you thought you had narrowed down. Seriously, who would have ever thought I would be seen in a long, to-the-knee sweater and matching leg warmers."

"Your own pregnancy shape is always a surprise when you spot yourself in a mirror or store window. For some reason, I guess because it comes on slowly month by month, you can't easily adjust to that big belly when you look at it squarely. Inside you are still your old body shape."

Physical Changes
Internal "Fluttering"
Have you felt that faint fluttering that makes you think of tiny bubbles being blown inside, or wings fluttering? Known as quickening, this marvelous sensation is your unborn child's growing life. Your practitioner may tell you that this indication of fetal movement is a wonderful way to determine how far along you are. If you are average, you'll detect these kicks, turns, flips, and pushes somewhere between the eighteenth and twentieth week. However, women who have already given birth can sense their baby's activity inside the womb as early as week 16 or 17 sometimes. According to spiritualists and some religious traditions, quickening sets the real beginning of a living human being.

Feeling Hot and Sweaty

Your metabolism works overtime during pregnancy. Like an overheated engine, your body is burning more calories even when you are simply sitting still. An increase in blood supply to the surface of your skin and all the raging hormones in your pregnant biochemistry add to the heat and sweat, too. To look and feel better, plan ahead.

- Don't dress in polyester clothes.
- Choose loose layers of cotton, so you can take off pieces as you start to perspire.
- Open windows at night to make sleeping more comfortable.
- Invest in a room air conditioner if you must.
- Hop in the shower to cool off.
- Drink water to replace all the fluids you are losing through sweat. You don't want to become dehydrated.

Nasal Congestion and Allergies

A stuffy nose, congestion, and postnasal drip are due to the high levels of estrogen and progesterone circulating, and the increased volume of blood reaching all your mucus membranes, making the lining of your respiratory tract swell. Experts say that this annoying side effect is harmless and will go away after your baby is born. Unfortunately, if you've always had problems with hay fever, sneezing, itchy, and teary eyes during particular allergy seasons, you may be even worse off. Yet, women with no previous history of allergies can also find themselves in this itching, sneezing, nose-blowing situation.

Speak with your doctor about remedies because there are safe medications available. Ask about taking extra vitamin C. If you are pregnant in the winter and the dry air is wreaking havoc on the delicate, sore skin of your nostrils, use a humidifier. In the meantime, try not to blow your nose too violently.

Taking Care of Yourself

RX for Nosebleeds

During pregnancy, for the same reasons many women suffer allergy-like symptoms, some women are prone to nosebleeds. If your nose does start to bleed, don't lie on your back or lean backward. Sit down, lean forward very slightly, and try blowing gently to remove any clot. If that doesn't work, stick a bit of wet cotton or sterile gauze in the bleeding nostril. Pinch your nose between your thumb and fore-finger with the gauze or cotton in place. Let your packing stay put for a few minutes and don't tug it out forcefully. Lean over a sink and wet it again when you think the bleeding has stopped. You can also try putting an ice pack on your nose. The cold should shrink the blood vessels and reduce bleeding. Nasal cauterization could be indicated if you are having recurring, severe nosebleeds. The nasal mucus membranes respond like your uterus with dilatation of blood vessels. Therefore, if you have a large vessel that is continu-ally bleeding, it may have to be cauterized by your practitioner.

An Itchy and Uncomfortably Painful Backside

You could develop hemorrhoids, which are swollen rectal veins around your anus. These itchy, sore, possibly painful bloody vessels can be a real trial, especially when you try to go to the bathroom. If you haven't already discussed your problem with the doctor, do it now. Don't be shy. In the meantime, sit down. Standing or shopping for hours at a time can put unnecessary pressure on your veins there. In fact, sit on an ice pack. Ask for a prescription for a cream. Most mild cases of hemorrhoids do go away after delivery. By straining to have a bowel movement, you put stress on the rectal veins, which can become blocked, trapping blood, turning itchy, painful, and perhaps even protruding from the anus. Near the end of your nine months of pregnancy, the pressure of the baby can also add to this condition.

Bleeding or painful hemorrhoids should always be brought to your doctor's attention right away. You may have developed a blood clot. In the meantime, here are a few other things you can do:

- ♂ Dab a little petroleum jelly just inside your rectum before going to the bathroom.
- ♂ Climb into a tub filled with warm water and soak your backside, especially if your hemorrhoids are protruding. To shrink them, sit on an ice bag or a washcloth soaked in ice water as soon as you get out of the bathtub.
- ♂ Keep medicated wipes called Tucks next to your toilet. Your obstetrician may also prescribe a suppository kit.
- ♂ To relieve constipation, try eating plenty of high-fiber foods and drinking more water. Exercise regularly and take your prenatal vitamins on a full stomach with plenty of water. The extra iron in some manufacturer's brands can be compounding the problem in your bowels. Don't take over-the-counter laxatives, however, and do speak with your practitioner.

Breathlessness

Are you having bouts of breathlessness? The reason you feel this way is that you have to increase your vital capacity when you are pregnant. Your oxygen requirements are higher and, as a result, you lose certain reflexes that make a nonpregnant woman breathe without concern. Most people breathe and never even think about it. When you are pregnant, this changes and the inability to breathe freely without thinking can happen even when you aren't even moving. Don't panic. Stay calm for a few minutes, and the sensation will go away. Meanwhile, pathological breathing is panting or breathing so rapidly that you start to feel faint. You can make yourself actually pass out. However, fainting is a method of protecting your body. After you faint, or lose consciousness, you'll start breathing easier. When breathlessness is caused by anemia, it's rapid breathing after some kind of exertion.

Sensitive Gums

Your gums can become extrasensitive and may actually bleed when you brush your teeth. Take it easy. Make an appointment with your dentist to have your teeth cleaned, but be sure to tell him or her that you are pregnant. If you need to have X-rays taken, make sure the dentist or technician covers your abdomen with a lead shield.

Sticky Discharge on Your Underpants

Have you noticed an increase in a thin, sticky, white discharge, similar to the kind you may have experienced just before your monthly period? If so, you've got a normal situation known as *leukorrhea* and not necessarily vaginitis, an infection. For some women, the leukorrhea increases to a point where they decide to wear a sanitary pad. Don't reach for a tampon, however. You don't want to risk introducing any germs into your vagina when you are pregnant. The discharge is really nothing to worry about even if it makes you feel uncomfortable. If you develop more annoying symptoms, such as pain, itching, redness, or swelling and a change in discharge consistency as well as color, call your doctor.

Vaginal Infections

Even if you haven't been one of those women prone to *vaginitis* (infections of the vagina), now that you are pregnant, some experts say that you are ten times more likely to develop one. Rest assured that simple vaginitis is not going to harm your baby. There are actually three types of vaginitis, according to obstetrician Harold Shapiro: *trichomoniasis*, *moniliasis*, and *bacterial vaginosis*. Moniliasis, or yeast infection, may be the most common one for expectant moms. You may also have a fungus called *Candida albicans* in your vagina. An overgrowth of this fungus will give you a case of cottage cheesy discharge, itching vulva, and red and swollen vagina. Let's face it, everything about your biochemistry is thrown off by the pregnancy, so why should the climate in your vagina be any different? Because there is concern about the unborn baby contracting the infection during the birth, you'll want to clear it up as soon as possible:

- Talk to your doctor and get tested. You need to rule out any sexually transmitted infections. A sample of your secretion may be needed to get the full story.
- Use an ice pack to soothe the itching. Applications of witch hazel may also relieve some of your frustrating and itchy symptoms.
- Boric acid capsules and ointments may be recommended.
- Eating yogurt, which contains lactobacilus-acidophilus, or the active cultures, could help. What you want to do is restore the right bacterial balance in your vagina and the yogurt actually has some of the very same organisms your body may need.
- Stay as clean and as dry as you can.
- Wear cotton underpants and avoid tight-fitting pants.

Heartburn

If you've been experiencing a burning sensation in your throat and chest, the cause is indigestion. The acid in your stomach is backing up into your esophagus. Your growing uterus isn't helping matters either as it grows and begins to push up on your stomach. Countless pregnant women have moaned and groaned their way through nine months of gastrointestinal upset. Hormones relax all your smooth muscle tissue, even the ones in your digestive tract. Food moves more slowly through your system. In fact, some people say that the slower it goes, the better off your baby may be because you are getting a lot more nutrient absorption. Avoid indigestion by:

- Skipping the greasy fries.
- Cutting down on fatty foods.
- Eating many small meals, instead of three square ones a day.
- Drinking lots of water. Although they may be sending you to the bathroom more than you like, fluids can help reduce that buildup of acid in your stomach.

- Avoiding eating just before you go to bed or are about to lie down to rest.
- Shopping for loose-fitting maternity clothes. Squeezing into your old jeans puts pressure on your stomach area.
- Trying an antacid such as Mylanta, Maalox, Riopan, or Milk of Magnesia. Tablets that could ease your upset are Gelusil, Rolaids, or Tums. Tums also supplies you with the extra calcium you need. Take two Tums after each meal and two before going to bed for a week. If you have also eliminated fried foods, your heartburn should be gone. If it's not, then you have to consult with your physician because your heartburn may not be a simple thing. You can actually end up with gastrointestinal bleeding from heartburn. "I have my patients use drugs like Pepcid and Zantac," says Dr. Berk. Work with your doctor to find the right medicine.
- Raising the head of your bed when you sleep or nap can help. Put six-inch blocks, or even a couple of sturdy books, under the mattress. Adding a pillow or two simply won't be as effective.
- Stay away from alcohol, cola, tea, coffee, chocolate, peppermint, and spearmint: these may relax the valve between the stomach and the esophagus, according to Richard Berkowitz, M.D., and Rosemary Wein, R.N., of Mount Sinai. This relaxation lets the contents of your stomach back up.
- Write down what you eat for a couple of days. You may be able to figure out which foods are the worst offenders. Although highly spicy meals, tomatoes, and citrus fruits or juices are known culprits, your own body may be reacting to another food group entirely.

Collect the following ten items your new family will treasure:

1. A photo of your current home

2. Photos of your extemded family

3. Political buttons or bumper stickers

4. A baby hat

5. Matches from favorite restaurant

6. Duplicates of special keys

7. Old driver's license/passport

8. Personal letter to the new baby

9. A copy of birth announcement

10. The newspaper from the baby's birth.

RECORD SHEET:
To Our Baby—A Message from Month Four

PHOTO CAPTION: *This picture was taken on_____. It shows*

_____.

Dear Baby:
This month has been quite an experience. The highlight was the ultrasound. Here's what you looked like inside me!

Important Reminders	Scheduled Activities "To Do"

Now is the time to . . .

- **Schedule/confirm your monthly checkup with your ob/gyn.** Record your next regularly scheduled checkup on the appropriate date in this planner!
- **Go to the appointment prepared.** Continue to track your symptoms. Draft a list of any questions you have. Bring both lists to your next doctor's appointment.
- **Schedule regular beauty treatments, such as a haircut, manicure, and pedicure.**
- **Schedule and plan regular "date nights" with the father-to-be—at least once a week.**

DAY 1

DAY 2

DAY 3

Scheduled Activities "To Do"	Important Reminders
DAY 4	*Now is the time to . . .* **Ask your doctor about amniocentesis.** When faced with an amniocentesis: • Pull your calendar out (How far along will you be when you receive the news?). • Consider all the issues (For instance, do you want to know the sex of your baby before birth, or would you rather wait?). • Discuss all your concerns with your practitioner before you schedule the test.
DAY 5	
DAY 6	

Now is the time to . . .

Write down your dreams.

Vivid and emotionally powerful dreams are very typical during pregnancy and immediately after delivery. Although no medical studies can confirm the connection between your elevated hormone levels and your very active dream state, experts do say that there is a link. Put a pad and pen next to your bed and record your dreams immediately upon awakening. Your "dream journal" can help you cope with unresolved issues about your pregnancy—and will make fascinating reading at a later date!

DAY 7

DAY 8

DAY 9

Scheduled Activities "To Do"	Important Reminders

DAY 10

DAY 11

DAY 12

Now is the time to . . .

Check your calcium intake.
   Are you getting at least 1,200 milligrams of calcium? Calcium is more important than ever, as your unborn baby is now developing bone and blood cells. Some experts believe that, in the second half of pregnancy, the unborn baby will use as much as thirteen milligrams of calcium per hour. The baby's nervous system, muscles, and teeth also depend on your calcium intake. Include calcium-rich foods in your diet, such as:

- Milk and dairy products.
- Sardines, mackerel, and salmon.
- Broccoli and other green leafy vegetables like kale, collard, and turnip greens.
- Calcium-enriched orange juice.

Important Reminders	Scheduled Activities "To Do"

Now is the time to . . .

Eat.

If you've been experiencing morning sickness, the nausea may ease up and disappear entirely.

Your appetite will increase and you can expect to gain from eleven to fifteen pounds, or 60 percent of your total maternity weight, in this trimester. Don't be a slave to that scale, however. Just concentrate on eating healthfully.

DAY 13

DAY 14

DAY 15

Scheduled Activities "To Do"	Important Reminders
DAY 16	*Did you know that . . .* **Your placenta is actually a multidimensional organ that takes care of the work of the lungs, kidneys, intestines, liver, and hormone-producing parts of the fetus's life?** There are two sides to the placenta: a maternal and a fetal. The placenta's marvelous biochemistry makes it possible for nutrients to pass and wastes to be removed. Your unborn baby's waste products, urine and carbon dioxide, are picked up in the placenta and eventually excreted through your own kidneys and lungs.
DAY 17	
DAY 18	

Important Reminders	Scheduled Activities "To Do"

Now is the time to . . .

Stay organized.
Among the pregnancy symptoms linked to the hormonal storm brewing in your body is a feeling that you are a bit more scatterbrained than normal. Your inability to remain clearheaded is normal and not lifelong. Some experts liken your foggy feeling to the same sensations you may have had at particular times of your monthly menstrual cycle. How to cope?

- Make lists for your essential to-dos.
- Reduce the stress in your life, if possible.
- Don't rush
- Don't expect more of yourself now than you would have been accomplishing every day even before you were pregnant.
- Stop aiming for 100 percent efficiency in everything you do.

DAY 19

DAY 20

DAY 21

Scheduled Activities "To Do"	Important Reminders

DAY 22

....
....
....
....
....
....
....
....
....
....
....

DAY 23

....
....
....
....
....
....
....
....
....
....
....

DAY 24

....
....
....
....
....
....
....
....
....
....
....

Did you know that . . .

Changes in skin pigmentation are normal?
Your nipples and the surrounding skin on your breasts may get darker in color. Meanwhile, a line running down the center of your stomach, called the *linea nigra*, might appear. Moles and freckles become more defined and darker. Don't worry. This isn't a sign of cancer. It just reflects an increase in skin pigmentation due to biochemical changes during pregnancy.

Important Reminders	Scheduled Activities "To Do"

Now is the time to . . .

**Ask your hospital
about siblings classes.**

If you have other children, you may want to enroll them in a class for siblings of newborns. Many hospitals have them these days. Enroll your child at any point from midpregnancy on. The arrival of a new sibling can be a joyous occasion for a young child if it's handled in a sensitive manner. Other ways to help children cope with a new baby:

* Involve them in the pregnancy from the start.
* Get them to help decorate the baby's room.
* Bring out your child's own baby scrapbook, or pictures, and reminisce about his or her birth.
* Give your child a special present when presenting the new baby.
* Set and keep a special time together, and continue to enjoy it later, after baby's birth, when baby is napping.

DAY 25

DAY 26

DAY 27

Scheduled Activities "To Do"	Important Reminders

DAY 28

....

....

....

....

....

....

....

....

....

....

....

DAY 29

....

....

....

....

....

....

....

....

....

....

....

....

DAY 30/31

....

....

....

....

....

....

....

....

....

....

....

....

A great idea . . .

Make a time capsule for baby.
A time capsule is a keepsake that your child will enjoy as he or she gets older. It is a way of telling your child that his or her birth was a very important occasion. It should include the happenings, excitement, and triumphs of the days when baby was in the process of being born . . . newspaper highlights, billboard's top 100 hits list—anything that conveys the popular culture and important issues and themes of the day. Also include personal mementos from mom and dad, and how you spent your time together—watching movies, menus from special restaurant dinners. To store these items, cover a box in baby wrapping paper, or, visit one of the many scrapbook stores that are starting to pop up all over. They carry a myriad of scrapbooks, boxes, and kits to help preserve special memories.

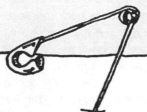

MONTH FIVE

Your notice other pregnant women everywhere, You can't sleep soundly on your stomach anymore, And you need a back massage . . .

TO DO THIS MONTH

- ☐ *Look fondly at your body.*
- ☐ *Think voluptuous, not fat.*
- ☐ *Write down new symptoms.*
- ☐ *Schedule a massage.*
- ☐ *Stand up straight and tall.*
- ☐ *Buy sunscreen and a hat.*
- ☐ *Rest during the day.*
- ☐ *Play with your hair care.*
- ☐ *Moisturize your skin.*
- ☐ *Go on a date with your mate.*

You've made it to month five, the middle month of pregnancy, the month when the reality of your new body sets in . . . You can't sleep soundly on your stomach anymore, and you need a back massage . . .you really show, now . . . everyone can see that you're pregnant, and you, too, notice pregnant women everywhere . . . more body-conscious than ever, and perhaps a bit self-conscious. Not all mothers-to-be look at their pregnant bodies the same way. Some regard their pregant body with fondness, remembering the fun they had with the amusing shape they were in, others, with misery, recall only how awful they felt about themselves, and how huge they believed they looked to the world. The difference is really attitude, and has nothing to do with actual weight gain. While it isn't possible to wish away any of the aches and pains of pregnancy, your state of mind can definitely affect the degree of your distress. A case of the emotional uglies will make you feel worse. That's why it's more important than ever before to take good care of yourself, and to encourage positive thoughts about your new shape. Try these helpful self-care practices:

- Substitute the word "voluptuous" for "fat" when looking at your image in the mirror.
- Schedule a massage.
- Practice standing up straight and tall.
- Buy sunscreen and a hat to protect your delicate skin from the sun's damaging rays.
- Rest during the day—you need it!
- Try some new hair styles.
- Shop for comfortable, but elegant shoes—they'll make you feel attractive, and, as your feet feel the effects of the additional weight, you may find you need wider or larger footwear to be comfortable throughout the day.
- Moisturize your skin; hormonal changes can cause extra dryness.
- Continue to write down any new symptoms.
- Go on a date with your mate.

This Month's Priorities

- ❏ Write down your symptoms.
- ❏ Monitor for diabetes.
- ❏ Track the fetal condition.
- ❏ Plan for life after the birth.

How Your Baby Grows

Your unborn baby may grow two more inches this month, increasing in length to anywhere from ten inches up to fourteen or fifteen. Your baby's weight also will increase, from six ounces up to a full pound by month's end. Hair is growing on his or her head. Teeth are developing, and minuscule tooth buds for permanent teeth are already there, too. The skin is still see-through, making the fetal blood vessels appear to glow. Silvery little bones are visible but starting to harden in this second trimester. The arms and legs are well formed, and the unborn baby can grip firmly with its hands.

A white greasy substance called *vernix* will soon protect the skin in its watery, womb environment. Secreted by tiny glands in the skin, *sebum*, an oily film, first appears before becoming waxy and thick to form the vernix. Like any marathon swimmer getting ready for a long-distance race, your unborn baby needs this greasy protection. (Babies born prior to their due dates sometimes come into the world with a coating of this cheeselike substance.) The limbs are still covered by the soft, silky hair known as lanugo, most of which will be rubbed off and disappear before birth.

Do you think talking to your baby now is silly? It's not. The fetus responds to noises from outside the womb. The fetus recognizes your voice and has actually been shown to startle at the sound of loud crashes or bangs. The sounds of your digestive tract and your heartbeat are heard clearly inside.

Fluttering, kicking, somersaulting, twisting, and turning, the unborn baby may be most active at predictable times. Rest and sleep are also on the daily fetal must-do list. In fact, some unborn babies have been known to respond to the rocking and gentle motions of their mothers long before they see the light of real day. This may explain why your baby sleeps more when you are active during the day. In the evening, with your feet up, finally relaxed in your favorite chair or propped up on the bed with a pile of pillows for comfort, you can't quite drift off or give in to your fatigue because it's exercise time in the womb! Have your mate stick around to see and feel the action.

What You Can Expect to Experience

Emotional Changes

One of the biggest emotional challenges facing moms-to-be during this trimester is adjusting to weight gain and changing body shape. With our society's emphasis on slim bodies, it's not surprising that some pregnant women feel fat and less attractive. The first step toward getting rid of any inferiority complex is to understand that such feelings generally come from faulty errors in logic. Here are some of these errors, and how to deal with them:

Error No. 1: The Medical Standard for a Perfect Pregnancy Weight Gain Is Reasonable

Twenty years ago, women were scolded if they gained more than eighteen pounds; yet, the American College of Obstetricians and Gynecologists (ACOG) still says that twenty to thirty pounds is ideal. A majority of women gain more than thirty pounds, according to nurse-midwife Lonnie Morris, who has been directing the Childbirth Center in Englewood, New Jersey, for more than twenty years. "Gains of twenty-five to thirty-five pounds have the best outcomes in pregnancy," Morris says. It's only when a woman gains more than fifty pounds that there is a need for her to worry that she will lose her figure.

Error No. 2: All Your Pregnancy Weight Gain Should Be in the Stomach Area

Wrong. You need to gain weight all over when you are pregnant to keep your balance, among other reasons. Some of these additional pounds may settle in your lower torso—on all of those hot spots of emotional upset for women: thighs, hips, buttocks. Rest assured, if your entire pregnancy weight gain were only in the stomach area, you would have a difficult time walking without falling forward.

Error No. 3: Pregnancy Is Something to Hurry Through and Hide

Obsessed with the exaggerated slimness of model figures, people in the fashion and garment industry seem to feel that pregnancy isn't a very pretty time of life. Many feel it a compliment to tell a woman expecting a baby that "you don't even look pregnant." But maternity and fashion are not mutually exclusive terms. Some of the most fashionable looks back in the fifties were A-line dresses with large collars (see Doris Day's wardrobe in the movie, "Pillow Talk.") Back in 1957, a friend of mine's mother, scared to tell her boss she was pregnant for fear of losing her job, didn't have to worry about finding plenty of clothes to wear—all designed for women who weren't pregnant. Make the most of your "new look."

Error No. 4: You Should Look Like the Fashion Models in Maternity Ads

Wrong. Usually, they are not pregnant. Pregnant faces, legs, and arms look fat when photographed; so many times, models "fake" looking pregnant with pregnancy pillows.

Physical Changes

By now, the top of your uterus has reached your navel. Put your finger there to see if you can feel it. Meanwhile, expect to continue experiencing some of the same symptoms that made your life difficult last month. Consider yourself normal if . . .

- **You have begun to experience occasional twinges of pain or dull aches in your lower abdomen.** Common between the eighteenth and twenty-fourth weeks of pregnancy, these simply mean that your uterus is growing, and the ligaments that support it on either side are being pulled and stretched. Don't turn quickly from your waist. Change your position if you sit for long periods. When you feel a tug, bend into where the pain is originating. Don't forget to tell your practitioner.

- **Your back aches—half of all pregnant women experience an achy back, which can begin somewhere in mid-pregnancy and continue right on up to delivery day and beyond.** As your weight distribution changes, so does the way you stand, sit, walk, and move. And all this can put strain on your back muscles. What also may begin to bother you during this fifth month is a condition called *lumbar lordosis*. The pain is caused by your spine curving forward, twisting itself to make space for the baby inside. The curving is caused by a substance called relaxin circulating in your body.

- **You're still constipated.**

- **You've got heartburn and indigestion indignities, such as bloating, burping, and flatulence.**

- *You may not feel like racing to find bathrooms as often with a need to urinate.* (Don't become too comfortable with this turn of events. Your need to urinate will increase again in the last trimester as the baby grows bigger and the pressure on your bladder makes you want to go all the time.)

- **You get dizzy and feel lightheaded.**

❀ **Your nose is stuffed up and drippy on occasion, as if you had allergies working out of season.**

❀ **You are incredibly hungry and find yourself desperately seeking treats at all hours of the day and night.**

❀ **You crave sleep, although you are not quite as sleepy as you were back in the very beginning of your pregnancy.** If you are finding it difficult to sleep face down now because of your growing belly, you may be frustrated.

❀ **You get headaches.** Hormonal changes are probably the real culprit here, although anxiety, fatigue, and hunger can also make your head pound in ways you've never known before. If you get migraines, they may either become your worst nightmare now, or disappear completely. Ask your practitioner for her or his recommendations for medicine to relieve them. Don't take aspirin.

❀ **You notice changes in the color of your skin, specifically a dark line down the center of your belly (linea nigra) and splotches on your face (chloasma).**

❀ **You are still sweating after all these weeks because of your speedy metabolism.** Even the palms of your hands get overheated at times.

❀ **Your breasts are still growing, and nipples may be getting darker.** In fact, your breasts produce colostrum, the first fluid your new baby will receive from you if you are breastfeeding. Made up of water, proteins, minerals, and anti-

bodies to protect a newborn, colostrum is thick and yellow early in pregnancy but becomes clearer and thinner later. You may have noticed some of it leaking from your breasts, especially when you are making love or are sexually excited.

- **You've gained at least six pounds.**
- **When you lie down or sit for a rest, your stomach doesn't stop moving, as your unborn baby tries out new movements and develops muscle.** Late evening is when fetuses are ordinarily most active.
- **Your fingernails may be soft and brittle because of the increased level of hormones.** Have your nails done by a professional manicurist.

Other typical changes during this trimester are:

- **Changes in your complexion:** Some women have a luminous "glow," from extra oils being released. Some women see blemishes disappear. If you have sensitive skin, however, all the hormones combined with tension can contribute to breakouts, rashes, allergies, dryness, or extreme oiliness.
- ***Stretch Marks:*** Almost all expectant mothers develop what are euphemistically called "stretch marks"—pink, reddish indentations or streaks in the skin. Breasts, hips, as well as the abdomen, are trouble spots. You may freak a little at first. Stretch marks are the response of your skin to the steroids that your body is putting out. You see this happen when someone is given cortisone and develops stria or white lines on the skin's surface. Young women who are just starting to menstruate can develop stretch marks, not from the skin doing any stretching, however, but from the steroids they are producing. Creams and oils will *not make stretch marks disappear, but time will.*
- **Dark Lines and Patchy Blotches:** You may notice changes in skin color, specifically that dark line down the center of your belly. You've always had a white line that runs

from your belly button down to the top of your pubic bone, but pregnancy hormones can make it turn darker, so its name, *linea alba*, is officially changed to *linea nigra* for these nine months. Don't worry, it will return to its nearly invisible, white state when you become a mother.

♂ **The Mask of Pregnancy:** Because the change in skin pigmentation shows up across your cheeks, nose, upper lip, and forehead, chloasma is commonly called "the mask of pregnancy." For dark-skinned women, the "mask" may appear lighter, and in light-skinned women, the pigmentation is darker. Researchers suspect that it is caused by an extra sensitivity to all the estrogen circulating in your body. Have you noticed that your freckles are darker? Are your moles standing out more, too? Estrogen is sending the pituitary gland in your brain a message to release more of the melanocyte-stimulating hormone (MSH). The MSH makes your skin secrete more of the skin pigment known as melanin.

What can you do about chloasma?

♂ Be patient. It will go away. This overheated state of skin pigmentation will gradually disappear after the birth.
♂ Direct sunlight can make discoloration worse, so don't go out in the bright sunshine without a hat as well as lots of sunscreen. Buy a sunblock especially for your face, with the highest number SPF you can find.

Taking Care of the Two of You

Monitoring for Diabetes

Sugar in your urine, especially during the second trimester, is not unusual. Fifty percent of all expectant moms show up with excess sugar. The fast-growing fetus demands lots of nutrients, and biochemistry simply can't keep up with the demands. When not enough insulin is produced, the excess sugar ends up in the kidneys. A routine urine test may indicate a high level of sugar in your system, which could mean that you are developing a type of diabetes known as *gestational*. If you've been feeling fine and sailing through these weeks, this news may come as a shock. Don't freak out yet. In many cases, a second urine test will show that this imbalance has disappeared because your body starts producing more insulin to take care of the excess sugar. If high sugar levels appear after a second urine test, your doctor may order a blood test to confirm the condition and a *glucose tolerance test (GTT)* to see if your problem is more serious. Glucose is simply a type of sugar, but too much of it in your body is not a good thing for you and your growing baby.

Is It Diabetes?

- Keep in mind that the way your body metabolizes sugar always undergoes a big change when you are expecting. In fact, normal pregnancies bring on a diabetic-like state, so a case of gestational diabetes now does not mean that you will have full-blown diabetes after the birth.
- Your doctor may arrange for you to speak with a certified diabetic educator so you can learn how to check your glucose level at home with a store-bought monitor.
- You may be placed on a special diet for diabetics.
- An ultrasound can check the growth and well-being of your baby. When it is uncontrolled, gestational diabetes alters the way your baby grows, increasing the size but hindering the maturity. In other words, you can have a big baby not physically ready or prepared for life. By measuring the fetal movement and breathing patterns, an ultrasound will ensure that growth is right on target for size.

Folate Checklist

Food	Serving Size	Amount (Mg)	Daily Value %
❏ Chicken liver	3.5 oz	770	193
❏ Breakfast cereal	½ to 1½ cup	100–400	25–100
❏ Braised beef liver	3.5 oz	217	54
❏ Lentils, cooked	½ cup	180	45
❏ Chickpeas	½ cup	141	35
❏ Asparagus	½ cup	132	33
❏ Spinach, cooked	½ cup	131	33
❏ Black beans	½ cup	128	32
❏ Burritos with beans	2 burritos	118	30
❏ Kidney beans	½ cup	115	29
❏ Baked beans (pork)	1 cup	92	23
❏ Lima beans	½ cup	78	20
❏ Tomato juice	1 cup	48	12
❏ Brussel sprouts	½ cup	47	12
❏ Orange	1 med	47	12
❏ Broccoli, cooked	½ cup	39	10
❏ French fries	Large order	38	10
❏ Wheat germ	2 tbsp	38	10
❏ Fortified white bread	1 slice	38	10

Tracking Fetal Movement

You may be asked to keep track of fetal movement. All unborn babies are different, and their activity can be erratic. When you are really busy, you may not even notice the kicking, shoving, twisting, and turning. In fact, fetal activity becomes more clearly defined and active only after Week 24 and up to Week 32. Some doctors suggest that you try to keep track of the movement by counting kicks or any swishing, fluttering, rolling, and turning at certain times of the day.

The old approach was to relax, lie back, and try to look at the clock in the middle of a busy day to catch your unborn baby kicking.

The object was to note at least ten movements, checking the time before and after, and writing it down. Experts believe that fetuses sleep in short bursts of twenty to forty minutes at a time, so if you were unlucky and caught yours during a neonatal nap, you were to try counting kicks later. Within a two-hour span, you were told to catch at least ten moves.

However, Dr. Howard Berk has a more modern approach for busy women anxious to count kicks. "In the world today, what woman has time to lie down to check her kick counts? Only when she is ready to fall asleep is this possible. During the day, she's either working, she's got other kids to take care of, she's providing transportation for her family, or she may even be writing a book. An active woman can't spend time lying down watching the clock."

Instead, choose four hours in the morning when you are active. You should feel four separate groups of movements within that time frame. You don't have to count specific kicks. What you are looking for is fetal movement.

Dr. Berk cautions, "I also don't recommend this until the end of a pregnancy or if a complicated situation exists. If you don't feel any movement at all during that four-hour period, then call your practitioner. A sonogram can be employed to watch the movement as well as a non-stress test. In the meantime, to try counting kicks at only twenty weeks is really too soon. You've almost just begun to feel the baby and what those little pats mean. Start your own modern-day kick counting at the end of month seven."

Monitoring the Fetal Heart Rate

You could be scheduled for a *non-stress test (NST)*. This test, done to measure fetal heart rate, can be done at any time after your unborn baby's heart starts beating and is not necessarily scheduled for your second trimester. When you move, your heart rate speeds up and so does your baby's. These ups and downs in fetal heart rate are considered a good sign. You'll be on a bed or examining table attached to the same kind of fetal monitor used during delivery. The belt is strapped around your abdomen. For about twenty minutes, every time you feel your baby move, you'll push a button. In some situations, the monitor detects the movement without your pushing a button. What the testers—and you, too—want to see is your baby's heart rate going up and then back down. If there is no change at all with the activity, fetal distress is suspected. Sometimes, a buzzer or vibrations are used to wake up a sleeping fetus. If so, your NST includes a fancy extra called vibroacoustic stimulation.

Other Tests to Determine How Baby is Growing

Other tests to determine how your baby is growing may be scheduled. If everything is proceeding along normally, your doctor may not even mention some of the other tests that make it possible to see your baby's progress.

- Your doctor may ask for a *Biophysical Profile (BPP)*. When you have an ultrasound combined with a non-stress test (NST), you end up with a BPP. Fetal heart rate, muscle tone, body and breathing movement, as well as the amount of amniotic fluid are all noted and included on your chart. Of course, your baby isn't breathing real honest-to-goodness oxygen yet, but he or she is making all the right moves. The fetus gets oxygen from your placenta. A score of eight to ten is normal. The test will take about a half-hour.

- If there is any concern about the baby, or if you are still pregnant at forty-one or forty-two weeks, the first thing you'll have is the non-stress test. If that test is not reactive, you could be asked to have *a stress test, or oxytocin challenge test (OCT)*, in which mild contractions are induced to see how the baby responds. The hormone pitocin will be injected to start the stress test. If the baby cannot maintain his heartbeat during a contraction, or if the heartbeat falls, this is an indication for immediate delivery, according to Dr. Berk.

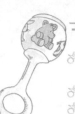

- Doppler velocimetry can measure blood flow to the umbilical cord.
- Fetal electrocardiography checks fetal heart rate.
- In a fetal scalp stimulation, someone actually puts pressure on, or pinches, the unborn baby's head.
- A sampling of blood may be taken.

Planning for Life After Birth

You're only five months into your pregnancy. You may feel as if you have plenty of time left to plan your post-pregnancy life, but the next few months will go by very quickly, and you don't want to have the added pressure of making significant decisions while you're being wheeled to and from the delivery room. By starting to think early about your options for work, household help, and baby care post-partum, you and your husband will be able to arrive at sound decisions for starting family life in an unhurried fashion.

To Work or Not?

For some women, an extended pregnancy leave is not an option. While some companies may hold a job for six months or longer, many others will not. You may find yourself in the position of having to decide whether to become a working mother or a stay-at home mom. If you would enjoy staying at home with your newborn, and can afford to, then that may be an easy choice for you to make. But the reality today is that many families depend on two incomes.

Some parents manage to adjust the particulars of their work life so that they can both work and still spend plenty of time with their baby. Here are some ideas on how to do this:

- *Ask if your company would consider a job-sharing arrangement.* In this scenario, you split a full-time job with another person who can do the same kind of work into two part-time jobs. This way, you both have more time to spend with your families—and the job still gets done in the same time frame.

- *Find out if your company allows for a flex-time option.* A forty-hour workweek might consist of four days per week at 10 hours each—or see if you can arrange a workday that begins earlier or ends later than usual.
- *Telecommute.* If your job is one that can easily be accomplished at home, ask if you can work from home—and come in only for important meetings, presentations, or the like. Working from home is every bit as challenging for a telecommuter as it is for an entrepreneur, so be sure you're up to it. If you're the type who's distracted by the need to vacuum over the need to finish a report, think twice before considering the telecommuting option. And remember, because you are at home, you will probably still need child care in order to get anything done—however, your baby can be cared for in your own home in your presence.
- *Hunt for a new part-time job.* There may not be much part-time work available in your field, but you might consider branching out into a related field. You just might find work that you enjoy even more than your old job!
- *As a last resort, you might consider a job where you can work evenings while your partner works days (or vice versa).* That way, one of you can be with the baby all the time. The drawback to this, though, is that you will rarely see each other. Extra care and effort will have to go into making sure that you keep lines of communication open between you, and that you spend time maintaining your own relationship.

Here are some things to look for during a visit to a daycare center:

1. Do the children at the center seem happy?

   _____

   _____

2. Do they look reasonably clean?

   _____

   _____

3. Are the rooms bright and airy?

   _____

   _____

4. Do they have natural light?

   _____

   _____

5. Is there a good selection of toys? Centers should have plenty of age-appropriate, safe toys that encourage creativity and motor development.

   _____

   _____

6. Is the center clean? In particular, check the bathrooms and food preparation areas. Do you detect a strong odor of urine anywhere?

   _____

   _____

7. Is there a safe outdoor play area?

   _____

   _____

8. Is the center thoroughly childproofed? Ask to see fire exits and first aid supplies.

_____

_____

9. Watch the staff interact with the children. Do the childcare providers seem attentive to the children's needs?

_____

_____

10. How noisy is the center? Happy kids do make noise—but total chaos is a problem.

_____

_____

11. How capable do the childcare providers seem at setting limits for the children? At resolving conflicts between the children?

_____

_____

12. Does the staff seem willing and eager to talk with you? Do they appear interested in getting to know your baby?

_____

_____

13. Are you meeting everyone who works at the facility, from the operator to instructors to clean-up help? You should be able to meet anyone who might possibly come into contact with your baby.

_____

_____

Daycare Options

If none of the above options are feasible, you will need someone to care for baby while you're both at work. You may need to start your search for a quality daycare situation—one that meets all of your expectations. Planning is the key to finding good daycare; taking the time to develop your plan well in advance of your baby's birth will eliminate additional stress later on.

Start checking out daycare possibilities as soon as possible—as early as your third month of pregnancy. Quality daycare is in high demand—and some daycare centers even have waiting lists months long. If you wait until after the baby is born, you may have trouble finding a daycare situation you feel totally comfortable with: waiting too long could mean you'll have to settle for less than your ideal.

Daycare Centers

Daycare centers are one of the most popular options for working parents. In a center, your child will be cared for in a group setting by adults who are trained in childrearing and child development issues. To begin checking into daycare centers,

- *Ask your state childcare or child welfare agency for a list of licensed centers.* (This is essential, because some unscrupulous daycare operators will say they are licensed when they are not. If you still have doubts or questions, you can contact the National Association for the Education of Young Children [NAEYC] for more information.)
- *Call each center for basic information, such as fees, space availability, hours of operation, staffing credentials, and visitation, vacation, sick day, and dropoff/pickup policies.*
- *Ask about the ratio of children to childcare providers.* A quality daycare center should care for infants in a separate room, away from toddlers and older children (who can present safety hazards to infants). Infant childcare providers at daycare centers should care for no more than three infants apiece, and two is an even better number. Also, you should ask about how many babies are kept in each room. More

than six infants in a room, whatever its size, can make for a chaotic, institutionalized setting (and you don't want your baby kept awake constantly from other babies' crying).

♂ *If the center checks out so far, you may want to schedule a visit.* Ask the center director when the older children generally nap, and avoid visiting at that time, since you'll want to see how well the childcare providers manage when most of the children are awake.

Once you have narrowed your choices down to one or two centers, ask for at least three references. Call them all and ask for feedback. If they do not give you glowing reports, look elsewhere.

There are many positive aspects of using a daycare center. In a good situation, your child will have other children of a similar age to play with, facilities that are expressly designed for his or her needs, childcare providers who are knowledgeable and experienced, and a wide variety of age-appropriate activities. Daycare centers can also be moderate in price, especially when compared to the cost of hiring a trained nanny.

However, if you are choosing childcare for a young infant, you may find daycare centers a bit institutional and potentially over-whelming for your baby. Another negative consideration is the issue

of staff turnover. Even good centers can experience a lot of staff turnover, and too many childcare providers in too short a time can interfere with a baby's long-term ability to form lasting attachments to other people. Finally, any time you take your child outside of your home for care, you are in for a certain amount of inconvenience. Depending on the age of your child and the center's requirements, you will need to have a diaper bag packed each day with diapers, wipes, bottles, bibs, one or more changes of clothes, etc.—and this, coupled with having to get your child fed, dressed, and ready (and getting yourself dressed and ready for your job), can make early mornings at your home a bit hectic.

Family Daycare

Unlike a daycare center, a family daycare provider cares for children in her own home. Often, one or more of the children in the group are her own.

Most states have licensing requirements for family daycare, but some providers operate illegally, either because they cannot meet the health, safety, or educational requirements of their state licensing agency, or because they do not want to declare their daycare income to the IRS (these will insist that you pay them in cash). If you live in a state that licenses family daycare operations, resist the urge to check out that nice, but unlicensed, childcare provider down the street, and only consider licensed childcare providers. However, since some state requirements are fairly minimal, it is important to check out even licensed family daycare situations carefully.

- Start your search by obtaining a list of licensed childcare providers in your area from your state childcare or child welfare agency.
- Ask friends and neighbors if they know of any good family daycare providers, and check to see if those people are on your list. Call those names first and ask if they have room for your child. It can be harder to find family daycare for an infant than for a toddler, since childcare providers typically can accept only one or two infants into their group. If

a provider is recommended but doesn't have room for your child in the near future, ask her to recommend someone who might.

Family Daycare Checklist

If a provider meets your requirements, make an appointment to visit her during the day. She may ask you to come during naptime, but make sure you see her in action while all the children are awake too. Spend some time there and check the following things:

- ❏ Is the house clean? The kitchen and the bathroom should be clean and sanitary. Also, check out the floor. Babies and young children spend a lot of time on the floor, so carpeting should be vacuumed frequently, especially if there are pets. Also, unless you are standing right next to the diaper pail, you should not detect a strong odor of urine anywhere.
- ❏ Is the house childproofed? You should see gates on the staircases, latches on kitchen cabinets, and covers on visible electrical outlets.
- ❏ Do the children look happy? Is the atmosphere calm? Does the provider seem relaxed or tense when she is dealing with the children?
- ❏ Is there a good selection of toys? Don't expect as many toys as you might find at a daycare center, but the provider should have at least a few age-appropriate, safe toys that encourage creativity and motor development, for both the infants and the older children. The provider may also allow you to bring over some of your child's own favorite toys and leave them there.
- ❏ Is there an outdoor play space? Is it safe and fenced off? If the provider does not have an outdoor play space, ask her where she takes the children for outdoor play.
- ❏ Finally, check at least three references—ideally, parents of children she cares for or has cared for in the past. If they don't seem enthusiastic about her, keep looking.

In a good family daycare situation, your child will spend his or her day in a homey atmosphere and will benefit socially by having other children to play with. If you stay with the daycare provider over the long term, your child may come to regard her as a second mom and be treated as part of the family. In many areas of the country, family daycare is also relatively inexpensive and a more economical option than are daycare centers. As with a day-care center, though, you sacrifice a certain amount of convenience when you take your children outside your home for childcare.

Childcare in Your Home

If you want your child to have one-on-one attention, childcare in your home can be a good choice. There are two basic types of home childcare providers: nannies and au pairs. While many people think the two are basically the same thing, the differences are significant.

Nannies A nanny takes care of your child in your home. She may live in or live out. Many nannies have formal training in child-care and child development. Others have no formal training and instead rely on life experience.

There are many agencies that will, for a fee, help you find a nanny. While agencies vary in their screening and training processes, they should, at minimum, do a complete background check of potential candidates (including a police check), provide you with references, and find you at least a couple of candidates to choose from. While agency fees vary, nanny agencies in larger cities may charge you fees of $1,000 or more (although, if your first choice doesn't work out, the next search may be on the house).

What if you don't want to pay a nanny agency? Ask your rela-tives, your friends, your neighbors, your hairdresser, or people at your house of worship if they have anyone to recommend. You can also place an ad in your local newspaper. Specify number of chil-dren, their ages, whether you want live-in or live-out care, whether the nanny will need a car, the town you live in, and the minimum amount of childcare experience you would prefer.

Nannies are in high demand in most areas, and you will need to offer a competitive salary. In 1997, live-out nannies working in a major metropolitan area earned $7-$12 an hour, depending on level of experience and whether their salary was paid through an agency. You will pay less if you can find someone who is willing to live with you (you'll need an extra bedroom for this option) and take part of their compensation as room and board.

Keep your expectations realistic. Outside of hands-on childcare, a nanny should be able to prepare your children's meals and perhaps do a little light housework that pertains to their care (like picking up toys or doing your children's laundry). She is not going to clean your house from top to bottom and cook gourmet meals for you while your baby naps.

Au Pairs Despite popular misconceptions, an au pair is not a nanny. She is typically a college-age student who comes to this country for a year to experience American culture. Au pairs agree to commit to living with a family for a year's time and provide childcare and light housework in exchange for room, board, a stipend, and sometimes tuition expenses.

If you are considering hiring an au pair, keep in mind that the program was not created to provide childcare for Americans. Instead, it was designed to provide a foreign living experience for young people. You should also keep in mind that in other countries, au pairs generally have fewer responsibilities than they are often expected to assume in this country, and rarely serve as the sole care providers for children while the parents are out of the house.

You will need to hire an au pair through an agency. The agency is supposed to do a thorough background check and provide you with references. It is also supposed to provide the au pair with a certain amount of childcare training, as well as CPR training. Make sure you know in advance exactly what experience and training you can expect an au pair to have.

While you will probably not have the opportunity to interview a potential au pair in person, you can ask some of the same questions you would ask when interviewing a nanny over the telephone. Try to get a sense of the person's experience and interests, and whether the person is interested in, and likes, children.

A main attraction of au pairs is cost. If you have an extra bedroom, this is almost always the cheapest childcare option short of your relatives. Even when agency fees and an au pair's transportation and tuition are factored in, costs rarely exceed $200 a week, plus room and board, for a maximum of forty-five hours of childcare and light housework.

While you should be aware that while you may end up with a wonderful, nurturing, experienced live-in childcare provider, you may also spend a year trying to train a homesick teenager in the rudiments of baby care.

Making Your Final Childcare Choice

The bottom line is, if you don't feel comfortable— if something about the daycare center or individual childcare provider bothers you, no matter how small or seemingly unimportant, you owe it to yourself to either address the issue or to move on to the next center or person on the list.

You should expect the following from any childcare provider:

- *Open communication.* Providers should give you frequent and complete updates about your child's progress and problems. If they keep you informed, you can develop ways to deal with problems and build on activities and accomplishments of the day.
- *Open access to their home or center.* Parents must be welcome to visit at any time, even without calling first. Providers should also allow parents to make a reasonable number of phone calls to check on their child's well-being, especially in the case of minor illness or separation anxiety. You and the provider should work out the best

times for these calls and determine in advance how many are reasonable.

☆ *Honesty and confidence.* Childcare providers shouldn't make commitments they can't or don't intend to keep. They shouldn't cover up problems or accidents that occur.

☆ *Acceptance of your wishes.* Providers should abide by parents' wishes on matters such as discipline, TV viewing, food, adult smoking, and toilet training. If providers feel that they can't abide by certain wishes, they should be candid about their inability to do so.

☆ *Advance notice of any changes.* Since it is often very difficult to find adequate alternate care, providers should tell parents well in advance if they are going to change their hours or prices—or if they plan to close down or limit the number of children in their care. Parents need at least a month's (or, better yet, six weeks') notice if they need to find a new care provider for their child. A center or family daycare provider should also clarify holiday schedules, so parents know which days are covered and which are not. Not every calendar holiday is a paid holiday for working parents. And except in the case of emergency, parents should be given at least two weeks' notice even if the provider won't be available on a non-holiday day.

☆ *No advice unless asked for.* Providers shouldn't criticize or advise parents on child rearing unless parents ask for their advice. If asked, they should offer advice in a noncritical way. Of course, if providers see something that is seriously wrong (i.e., signs of child abuse, neglect, or malnutrition), they should discuss the problem with the parents, and, if necessary, contact the proper authorities.

☆ *Assurance that everyone in contact with the child is properly trained and/or supervised.* This includes screening of custodial help, training and supervising transportation workers, and assurance that anyone who visits has been cleared for entry.

RECORD SHEET:
To Our Baby—A Message from Month Five

PHOTO CAPTION: This picture was taken on_____. It shows

_____.

Dear Baby:
I've been having the most peculiar dreams. This was the strangest one. What do you think it means?

_____
_____
_____
_____
_____
_____
_____
_____
_____
_____
_____

Important Reminders	Scheduled Activities "To Do"

Now is the time to . . .

- **Shop for moisturizing soaps and skin treatments.** Your skin is changing, getting drier, so it's important to choose soaps and cleansers carefully. You may even want to avoid soap on your face completely. Use plenty of moisturizer on your face as well as your belly, but make sure that the first ingredient listed on the container is water, not oil.
- **Buy support stockings.** Combat swollen limbs and feet, and fatigued legs. Wear support hose or leotards. When you sit down, elevate your feet high enough so the blood rushes back into your body. Can you raise the bottom of your bed mattress? Even a few inches can help. Don't sit cross-legged. Ask your practitioner for recommendations.

Don't forget to . . .

- **Schedule/confirm your monthly checkup with your ob/gyn.** Record your next regularly scheduled checkup on the appropriate date in this planner!
- **Go to the appointment prepared.** Continue to track your symptoms for your next doctor's appointment.

DAY 1

DAY 2

DAY 3

Scheduled Activities "To Do"	Important Reminders

DAY 4

....
....
....
....
....
....
....
....
....
....

DAY 5

....
....
....
....
....
....
....
....
....
....
....

DAY 6

....
....
....
....
....
....
....
....
....
....
....

Now is the time to . . .

Plan a vacation. Middle months of pregnancy can be an excellent time to escape from your routine, especially if you are no longer experiencing morning sickness, and you have more energy.

Mention your travel plans to your practitioner, especially if you plan to be far away from your home, or out of the country. You may need to take a copy of your prenatal medical records with you. Also, think about the following:

- On the plane or train, get up and move around every couple of hours, especially if you expect to be in transit for a long time. If you are going by car, stop and walk around.
- Think comfort when you pack and dress.
- Plan smart eating strategies so you don't upset your already sensitive digestive tract. Put crackers, snacks, water, or juice in your travel bag.
- Eat balanced, nutritious meals when you are away so you don't upset your already sensitive digestive tract.
- If you've been plagued with constipation, take foods with fiber along, as well as plenty of water to help you stay as regular as possible. Put a box of prunes in your suitcase, for instance.

Important Reminders	Scheduled Activities "To Do"

Now is the time to . . .

Keep your blood circulating to avoid varicose veins.

During pregnancy, the pressure inside the veins in your legs is three times what it is normally. If you are overweight, if you are up on your feet for hours on end, if this is your second or third pregnancy, or if the tendency runs in your family, then those poor veins are likely to become swollen and painful. You need to improve circulation, so blood doesn't collect in your legs. To do this:

• Gently circle your ankles and feet whenever you can.
• Take up swimming or aquacize. The water will support your pregnant weight and make you feel more buoyant than when you are on land. In the water, leaning against the side of the pool, raise your leg to hip level and make small circles in front and to the side. Then, move to the next leg.

DAY 7

DAY 8

DAY 9

Scheduled Activities "To Do"	Important Reminders

DAY 10

DAY 11

DAY 12

Now is the time to . . .

Get Enough Sleep

By the fifth month, your new, rounded shape makes it a bit difficult for you to sleep in any old position—especially not on your stomach.

- Treat yourself to new pillows.
- Try several arrangements to make yourself more comfortable. Look for one of the new full-body pillows.
- Open the window to allow more fresh air into your bedroom if the outside temperature is pleasant.
- Take a warm bath before you go into bed.
- Have a light snack in the evening so hunger doesn't wake you.
- Don't drink any liquids after your dinner except a glass of warm milk. This tactic may cut your trips to the bathroom—tryptophan, a sedating substance in milk, might help.
- Exercising can also help tire your muscles so you are ready to fall asleep.
- Finally, if you find yourself tossing, turning, and uncomfortable about even being in bed, get up and do something that is fun. Try to make up lost sleep at night with a nap during the day.

Important Reminders	Scheduled Activities "To Do"

Now is the time to . . .

Check your vitamins. Are you getting enough folic acid? There may be a relationship between the B vitamin found naturally in fruits, green leafy vegetables, dried beans, peas, and whole-grain products, and skin pigmentation problems. Folic acid, the synthetic form of folate, is undoubtedly in your pregnancy vitamin arsenal, but when you discuss chloasma with your doctor, you might want to mention this aspect. Recent reports indicate that all women of childbearing years need at least 400 micrograms of folic acid, and, during pregnancy, you ought to have at least 800 micrograms a day.

Not only is folic acid critical to your health, but also a lack of this essential nutrient has been linked to brain and development problems in babies. In a new folic acid fortification program required by the Food and Drug Administration (FDA), manufacturers are being asked to add this vitamin to flours, breads, corn, grits, rice, and even noodle products. Some breakfast cereals are already fortified with folic acid.

DAY 13

DAY 14

DAY 15

Scheduled Activities "To Do"	Important Reminders

Now is the time to . . .

DAY 16

DAY 17

DAY 18

Change Your Hair Care Routine.
You put your hand to your hair
and it doesn't feel the same
anymore. Not only has the texture
changed from normal, oily, or dry
to some other category altogether,
but also you may have noticed
that it feels thicker. In fact, you
probably do have more hair on
your head than you did five
months ago. When you are not
pregnant, all women tend to lose
about 100 hairs a day. This is
normal. When you are expecting,
the hair stops falling out until after
the birth. Your thickened mane is
not the result of growing more hair
but of not losing as much each
day.

- Experiment with new
  shampoos and conditioners—
  for instance, if you've always
  used a shampoo for normal,
  oily, or dry hair, it's time to try
  something else. Don't stick
  with the same brand for
  months and months. In fact,
  don't rub the conditioner into
  your scalp. Try applying it only
  to the ends of your hair before
  rinsing.
- Wash your hair more
  frequently, but be careful not to
  dry it out.

Important Reminders	Scheduled Activities "To Do"

Questions and Answers . . .

A vegetarian diet?

A vegetarian diet during pregnancy requires careful monitoring. Be careful that you are eating a variety of protein-rich foods and lots of fruits and vegetables daily. Vegetarians who also avoid milk as well as eggs, ought to pay special attention to protein servings and calcium intake. If you are careful, your baby will be getting all the necessary nutrients. You may also need to take an iron supplement, however, because human beings have a difficult time absorbing the iron they need from plant sources. If your practitioner has recommended prenatal vitamins, iron is a mineral you are getting daily. Have a serious discussion with your practitioner or a nutritionist to talk about your diet and how it will affect the baby's growth.

DAY 19

DAY 20

DAY 21

Scheduled Activities "To Do"	Important Reminders

DAY 22

....
....
....
....
....
....
....
....
....
....
....

DAY 23

....
....
....
....
....
....
....
....
....
....
....

DAY 24

....
....
....
....
....
....
....
....
....
....
....

Do you know . . .

How to find a nurse-midwife?
Contact the American College of Nurse-Midwives, 1522 K Street, NW, Washington, DC 20005, and send a self-addressed, stamped envelope for their reply. (Web site: *http://www.midwife.org*).

Questions And Answers . . . .

Food poisoning makes me awfully nervous, especially now that I'm pregnant. Should I be worried?

Millions of bacterial food poisonings are reported every year, and outbreaks of food contamination can be scary now that you are eating for two. But most cases of food poisoning are not fatal, even though they can make you feel positively terrible. The foods most likely to become contaminated are meat, poultry, fish, shellfish, and unpasteurized milk. When you prepare food, remember the following rules:

- Wash up always and often.
- Hands, kitchen counters, and utensils should always be immersed in hot, soapy water before, after, and even in-between meal-making steps.
- Toss that damp, used, dish cloth right into your laundry bin because it can promote bacterial growth.
- Wash sponges thoroughly in hot water and don't keep them forever.
- Never let food sit on a counter or dinner table for more than two hours if the temperature of the food is between 45 and 140 degrees Fahrenheit.
- Refrigerate or freeze leftovers promptly.
- If food is discolored or smells funny, dump it.
- If a can or container has been leaking or is swollen, throw it away.

DAY 25

DAY 26

DAY 27

173

Scheduled Activities "To Do"	Important Reminders

DAY 28

....
....
....
....
....
....
....
....
....
....
....

DAY 29

....
....
....
....
....
....
....
....
....
....
....
....

DAY 30/31

....
....
....
....
....
....
....
....
....
....
....
....

Did you know that . . .

Your expanding belly will be measured and palpated (gently poked, pushed) again and again?

- By 32 weeks, the fundus, or the top of your uterus, is well above your belly button and putting pressure on your ribs and diaphragm.
- Do you realize that by the end of your ninth month, that versatile organ will have expanded in size to 500 times what it was before you got pregnant?
- In weight gain alone, your uterus goes from about an ounce-and-a-half to thirty ounces.

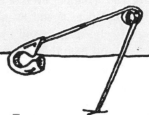

MONTH SIX

Itchy belly, nightly foot cramps,
Getting dressed in frustrated frenzy,
Preoccupied, flooded with fear,
You wonder, "Is this really me?"

TO DO THIS MONTH

☐ *Exercise: Walk, swim, stretch!*

☐ *Eat five servings of fruits or veggies a day.*

☐ *Sign up for childbirth classes.*

☐ *Plan a romantic occasion.*

☐ *Bring up your fears with friends, family, experts, and other moms.*

☐ *Browse in a baby store.*

☐ *Make a list of must-have infant essentials.*

As a very pregnant mother-to-be, this is the month when you begin to sense a certain, well, loss of privacy. "How are you feeling?" everyone, sometimes even strangers, ask you over and over again. Even people who haven't met you before seem to be magnetized by your belly— some may even walk right up and feel it! Most people don't really want to know about how all of those pregnancy "side effects" make you feel—your abdominal gas, signs of varicose veins, your aversion to apricots, or craving for pasta hardly make for fascinating conversation, except perhaps to other expectant moms. Keep in mind that you have a perfect right to feel violated and emotionally vulnerable. You can also simply say, "No thanks" to the suggestions from strangers.

In the meantime, you must find a way to deal with various discomforts—an itchy belly, nightly foot cramps, being preoccupied with fears about the remaining months of pregnancy and the impending delivery. Thankfully, your energy may very well be high right now, and you feel so inspired you think you can do anything . . . perhaps even decorate the baby's room in one day. Calm down, and don't put pressure on yourself to be wonder woman. To stay on an even keel, keep on

♂ Exercising: Walk, swim, stretch!
♂ Eating five servings of fruits or veggies a day.
♂ Planning romantic occasions with your spouse.

This Month's Priorities

❏ Bring up your fears with friends, family, experts, and other moms.
❏ Browse in a baby store and start planning baby's room.
❏ Make a list of must-have infant essentials and start stocking up on them.
❏ Start thinking of names.

Address Your Fears and Concerns

It's only natural to be afraid. You are heading into unknown territory. You may be lucky and have the shortest labor and delivery on record. Then again, you may spend hours confined to a small space in a situation in which there is no turning back. All those authorities—experts, authors, currently and formerly pregnant women—try to sound comforting, as they put the pain of childbirth into some kind of self-controllable package you will manage. Yet, thousands of years of history, literature, and books tell you otherwise. Terrible screams and agonizing labor pains accompany the natural act of birth. Your fears are very legitimate, so don't let anyone tell you to set your worries aside. Instead, get prepared. Yes, you are going through a time of vulnerability, dependency, and personal upheaval, but the chances of childbirth killing you or your baby are really minimal. You are going to survive and thrive. The pain? Let's just say, it's do-able, and you'll learn what to do when it starts. In the meantime, start collecting childbirth tales from all the women in your family. From this homework assignment, you may find similarities that will prepare you in a very personal way.

Start Planning Baby's Room

In the animal world, the female prepares a special place for her young shortly before birth. In this "nest," she gives birth, and, at the same time, provides a safe haven for her young to rest and grow in. In terms of your new baby's "nest," you and your partner will have the unique opportunity to create baby's first world outside of the womb—a place for it to dream, to experience, and to grow.

Since calm surroundings are so critical to a newborn's development, you should first give some serious thought to the location of the baby's room: Will it be on the same floor as your bedroom? If not, how will you monitor the room—with an audio or video monitor? Will the baby's room be near a busy, noisy street, or will it be facing a backyard where there is nothing but the sound of crickets?

Planning the best location for your baby's room is the starting point in designing the nursery. Once you have decided on the space, then you can begin filling the room with plush toys and cool designs. Before you rush out to choose the décor, write down the room's dimensions; then, when you're at the baby furniture showroom, you'll have a clear idea of what pieces will fit. Such planning with regard to location and size of the baby's room will save you infinite amounts of time—and heartache—if the motif you like doesn't fit well within the parameters of the room.

Choosing a particular décor depends on a few variables, such as how much you want to spend, how much space you have for the baby's room, and whether you know for certain if it's a boy or a girl. The best option is to go with something that's generic enough for both sexes; you can always add more gender-specific items after the birth, in addition to personalized items with baby's name printed on them. Good gender-neutral colors are greens, yellows, purples, and reds.

Creating just the right aura or atmosphere for your baby's room can be one of the most exhilarating things for you to do in preparation for the "Big Event." It is, after all, one of the few things you actually have control over in this birthing odyssey. A nursery invites creativity and use of the imagination. But keep these practical points in mind, too:

- Choose a nontoxic, washable paint or a washable, vinyl wall-covering for the walls
- Buy outlet covers to "baby proof" all electrical outlets
- Choose window coverings that can be easily cleaned and that are adjustable, such as venetian or vinyl blinds or shutters; "tie up" any dangling cords—they can endanger your baby when she grows to be a toddler

☞ Avoid buying cribs or furniture with protruding knobs or wide spaces between slats; your growing child can easily get his head caught in the spaces or "hang" herself by catching a piece of clothing on a knob.

Crib Safety Checklist

Since cribs are the only juvenile product manufactured for the express purpose of leaving a child unattended, extraordinary measures must be taken to ensure that a crib is as safe as possible.

❑ CORNER POSTS: Corner posts should be the same height as the end panels, and NOT extend above the end panels. Remove corner post extensions by unscrewing, or sawing off, and sanding smooth. Children's clothing catches on corner post extensions, resulting in strangulation.

❑ PROTRUSIONS/CATCH POINTS: A crib should have no protrusions of any kind on the inside or outside of the crib on which a child could get caught and strangle.

❑ SLATS: Space between slats must be less than $2^3/_8$" and no slats should be missing. Children attempt to squeeze feet first through wider slats, but their heads get caught, resulting in strangulation.

❑ CRIB HARDWARE: All screws, bolts, and hardware must be in place and tight to prevent the crib's collapse. The hardware and the crib should be smooth and free of sharp edges, points and rough surfaces. A child's activity can cause the crib to collapse, trapping and suffocating the child.

❑ MISSING/BROKEN PARTS: Before each assembly, and weekly thereafter, inspect crib for damage to hardware, loose joints, missing parts, or sharp edges. Do not use the crib if any parts are missing or broken. Do not substitute parts.

❏ CHILD'S HEIGHT: When a child first climbs out of the crib or is 32 to 35 inches tall, he or she has outgrown the crib and should sleep in a bed. In a full-size crib, the top rails of drop-sides, when raised, should be at least 26 inches above the top of the mattress support. The top rail of a lowered side should be at least 9 inches above the mattress support to prevent falls.

❏ DROP-SIDE(S): Must must hold securely in a raised position; must require two distinct actions or a minimum force of ten pounds with one action to release the latch or lock.

❏ END PANELS: Be sure end panels and sides extend below mattress support at its lowest position. A child can strangle by becoming trapped in the gap between mattress and end panels or sides.

❏ CUTOUTS: Cribs with cutout designs in end panels must not be used. A child can strangle by becoming entrapped in the cutout.

❏ TEETHING RAIL: Remove or replace if damaged or loose.

❏ PAINT: Cribs built before 1978 may have a higher lead content than current regulations allow. When using an older crib, be sure to strip off all the old paint and repaint with a paint designated for baby products. All wood surfaces should be free of splinters, cracks and chipping.

❏ PLASTIC BAGS: Do not use plastic bags or plastic material for mattress covers. Children suffocate when plastic material clings to the face.

❏ CRIB PLACEMENT: The crib should be located with safety in mind. Avoid placing it near any lamps, dangling cords or ribbons, windows, fans, heaters, or climbable furniture.

❏ INSTRUCTIONS: Must be provided with every new crib, and shall be easy to read and understand. These instructions shall include information on assembly, maintenance, cleaning storage, and use. Read all instructions before assembling the crib. Keep instructions for future use.

Crib Bedding Safety Checklist

❏ MATTRESS: It must fit snugly so that two adult fingers cannot fit between the mattress and the crib side. Baby may slip into wider gaps and suffocate.

❏ MATTRESS SUPPORT: It must not be easily dislodged from any point of the crib; a 1988 standard states that the mattress support must be able to withstand a 25-pound upward force from underneath the crib; it is meant to keep all four mattress support hangers securely attached to the headboard and baseboard of the crib; failure of even one hanger can cause the mattress to sag in the corner and pose an entrapment hazard.

❏ BUMPER PADS: These should be attached securely to all sides of the crib with at least six straps; excess length of straps should be cut off; must fit snugly into all four corners; there should be no gaps between the bumper pads and the crib sides; must never be used to offset improper spacing between slats; should be removed when a child is able to stand or kneel and move around the crib. Bumper ties should be nine inches or less.

❏ CRIB SHEETS: Be sure the sheet fits securely in all corners and sides. Check carefully for shrinkage after each wash. A child will pull poorly fitted sheets loose and become entrapped.

❏ PILLOWS: Do not put pillows in crib with baby. Infants may suffocate from soft spots. Toddlers will use pillows to climb out of the crib.

❏ CRIB GYMS AND MOBILES: Along with all other hanging cords, these must be removed when baby is able to push up on hands and knees.

Portable and non-full-size cribs:
❏ Should not be substituted on a permanent basis for regular full-size cribs. Not all non-full-size cribs are portable. Some

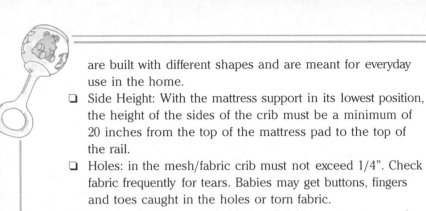

are built with different shapes and are meant for everyday use in the home.

- ❑ Side Height: With the mattress support in its lowest position, the height of the sides of the crib must be a minimum of 20 inches from the top of the mattress pad to the top of the rail.
- ❑ Holes: in the mesh/fabric crib must not exceed 1/4". Check fabric frequently for tears. Babies may get buttons, fingers and toes caught in the holes or torn fabric.
- ❑ Mattress Pad: in a mesh fabric crib, this must not exceed one inch.
- ❑ Never use additional mattress or padding. A child will suffocate when caught between the side of the crib and mattress pads.
- ❑ Fold Down Sides: Never leave an infant in a crib with the crib side down. The baby will roll into the space between the pad and loose mesh and suffocate.
- ❑ Folding cribs: All latches must work automatically to prevent the unintentional collapse of the crib. Babies die when entrapped in the "V" of an unintentionally collapsed crib.
- ❑ Check latches on the top rail before each use to be sure the latches have automatically locked into place.
- ❑ Catch Points: The crib must be free of protruding rivets, metal nuts or bolts. No knobs or wing nuts on the outside legs of the crib. Babies get clothing caught and strangle.

Checklist for Infant Essentials

- ❑ Toys that stimulate baby's brain or senses. Newborns enjoy contrast (such as black and white stripes and checkerboards); they can't identify pastel colors until six months old.
- ❑ Clothes: You'll need five or six undershirts (both full-snap and half-shirt varieties), nightgowns with pull strings at the bottom, and nonflammable sleepers or rompers with cov-

ered feet. You will also need at least four pairs of socks or booties (depending on the climate), one sweater or light jacket, two to four waterproof diaper covers, and one snowsuit (again, depending on the climate or the time of year). Additional clothes may be purchased in the 12- to 24-month size range (3- to 6-month clothes don't last long on a growing baby).

❑ Bath time items: You'll need a plastic bath tub or tub liner, two to four bath towels (preferably with a hood) or receiving blankets, three to four washcloths, sterile cotton balls, and alcohol (to keep the umbilical cord area clean until it heals). Toiletries for baby, including baby shampoo, lotion, a hair brush, and baby nail scissors. With shampoo and cleaning products, stick with brand-name, hypoallergenic items—you never know what sensitivities the baby will have.

❑ Sleepy time items: You'll need a crib set (including a bumper pad, three to four fitted sheets, and two comforters), a bassinet sheet (if you're using a bassinet), waterproof crib liners, a light blanket or sheet for cover, and a music box or mobile.

❑ Eating time items: You'll need four to six bottles (in both 4- and 8-ounce sizes for water, breast milk, formula, or juice), a bottle brush, a bottle rack (for easy—and sterile—dishwasher cleaning), six to eight bibs and burping cloths, and, if nursing, at least two nursing bras, breast pads and a breast pump (either manual or electric), and pacifiers.

❑ Changing time items: You'll need to stock your changing table with four or five undershirts or stretchies, petroleum jelly, baby wipes (alcohol free and hypoallergenic), a thermometer, a nasal aspirator, a pair of baby nail scissors, cotton balls and swabs, washcloths, diaper rash ointment, and, of course, hundreds of diapers!

Baby Equipment Checklist:
What You Need to Buy or Borrow

Now that you've got the baby's room decorated, you'll need to fill it with some major pieces of equipment. But with all of the equipment out there, it's hard to know what you absolutely need and what's optional.

Here are some general guidelines that will help you determine which items you really need to have in your baby's life:

- ❑ Bassinet or cradle: Optional. Some parents feel better when the baby is sleeping closer to their bed; that's why bassinets or cradles work so well in the first few weeks after birth. On the downside, you may spend a lot of money for something the baby can stay in only a short period of time (up until the third or fourth month). The bassinet or cradle doesn't replace the crib by any means. A 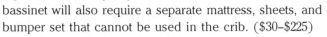 bassinet will also require a separate mattress, sheets, and bumper set that cannot be used in the crib. ($30–$225)
- ❑ Crib with mattress: Required. Whatever your taste in crib furniture, try out the floor model to see how easily the side rail comes down. This is an important feature: Look for ease of use and safety for the baby. Most makes and models conform to U.S. standards; check labels to be certain. In the crib itself, look for the following features: adjustable mattress heights, wheels, and the ability to convert to a toddler bed, if you are not planning on having other children. ($200–$600)
- ❑ Mattresses for cribs come in foam or innerspring options. They need to fit the crib properly (check dimensions) and should be covered with a waterproof cover. Foam mattresses

are lighter and easier to change than innerspring mattresses; also, they tend to be more economical. ($50–$200).

❑ Cribs also require fitted sheets, a bumper, and a cotton or wool blanket. Bedding accessories such as a dust ruffle or matching comforter are optional. ($50–$200)

❑ Stroller: Required. Carriage strollers are beautiful in appearance but can be heavy in reality. A carriage stroller is defined by the feature of allowing the baby to rest in a flat, horizonal position. The seat is supported by a frame that moves on four wheels. Large, set wheels allow for a smoother ride, and are recommended for mothers planning on lots of walking activities. Carriages set on smaller, swiveling wheels are better suited for quick turns and shopping. Carriage, or full-size, strollers are recommended for at least the first six months, as the baby will need to fully recline. Carriage strollers also usually come with some sort of basket—either mesh or a wire rack—that is handy when hauling lots of extra items, or for shopping excursions. The size of the basket is often a selling feature. These strollers can weigh as much as 25 pounds, so consider how much you can lift in and out of your trunk before purchasing.

❑ Umbrella strollers are designed for portability. They are completely compact, and fold into themselves for easy storage. These strollers do not typically recline to a flat position. However, they can weigh as little as seven pounds, and are great for traveling. They usually do not come with a basket attachment.

❑ The combination stroller/car seat is useful, and especially good for first-time moms, since it covers all the stages of growth to toddlerhood and is multipurpose. ($25 umbrella to $425 top-of-line carriage)

❑ Car seat: Required by law. You have the option of buying a car seat that is strictly for infants (rear-facing only, and handles an infant up to 20 pounds) or one that is for both

infants and toddlers (can convert to front-facing and holds an infant or a toddler up to 45 pounds). The benefit of buying one at a time is that you can make the toddler seat purchase to accommodate needs you know your child has; for instance, if he or she likes to look at books while in the car, a booster-type car seat for toddlers is what you'll need. If it's sheer economy you're going for, however, a combination infant/toddler car seat will probably do the trick. Keep in mind that some of the combination seats lack portability—an important consideration for some. You must have a car seat to take baby home from the hospital, and most states require that babies ride in approved car seats for travel by car or airplane. In sedans, or cars with airbags in the front passenger seat, any carseat must be placed in the back seat of the car. ($35–$80)

❑ Changing table, or dresser/changing table combo: Optional—but extremely useful. Some new mothers prefer changing their babies on a table. You may, on the other hand, feel more comfortable changing baby on a floor mat. Either way, you're going to need a place to store baby's clothes and diaper paraphernalia; so decide which method will work best for you as soon as you can. In the worst-case scenario, if you choose later on not to use a changing table, you'll have a lovely piece of furniture that you can resell later. ($35–$400)

❑ Baby carrier: Optional—but useful. These kangaroo-like carriers strap around your waist and shoulders and hold baby close to your chest. They are very useful when baby is still too small for a stroller, and they are amazingly easy to tote baby around in. And dads can get that "bonding" feeling from carrying baby around. ($15–$70)

❑ Playpen or porta-crib: Required. Baby needs a safe place to play during the daytime, especially when you're busy. You can choose from either a stationary fold-up playpen or a porta-crib. The obvious advantage with the porta-crib is its ability to be transported to Grandma's or to any other visiting spot on baby's busy schedule. Whichever style you choose, stock the playpen with soft, safe toys. ($45–$175)

❑ Rocker: Optional—but, oh so nice. There's nothing in the world like soothing a crying baby by rocking it back to sleep. You can choose either the old-fashioned wooden high-back rocker, or the more modern (and some say more comfortable) glider with ottoman variety. ($200–$500)

❑ Baby monitor: Optional. For years, mothers and fathers have been able to raise children without these types of products. And let's face it, you should always be close enough to monitor the baby yourself. However, they may occasionally come in handy. There have been some product recalls and problems associated with monitors, so it's worth looking into before making a purchase. Check out Consumer Reports before buying audio or video monitors. Definitely stay away from used or older models unless you're absolutely certain they're safe. And if you have portable phones already, make sure the monitor is compatible. ($45–$200 for video monitors)

❑ Sling carrier: Optional. Sling carriers keep baby in a good position for breastfeeding and are useful for carrying baby around the house with you as you go about your household duties. You can buy one of these used (and in good condition) at a consignment store, or you can purchase one new and resell it later at a consignment store. If you have a history of back trouble, this item is a skip. ($15 used–$40 new)

❑ Backpack: Optional. Some parents are more outdoorsy than others; if you like hiking in the park with baby, this is a terrific product for you. If, on the other hand, your major explorations take place in the mall, it's better to have a carrier that keeps baby in front of you. Backpacks are convenient; yet they can be a little dangerous

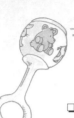

since baby can't tell you if a branch is about to hit his or her face. Backpacks cannot be used with newborns. ($40–$75)

❏ High chair: Required. Although you won't need it at first, since baby can't even hold his head up until about three months, you will eventually get lots of use out of your high chair. Baby does need to be confined during feeding time, and high chairs accomplish this most safely. Plus, there's a tray to protect you from wearing all of the food baby doesn't take a liking to. The tray will also serve as a "finger food" testing ground for baby. ($45–$200)

❏ Booster seat: Optional—but nice to have. After about six months, baby will be able to sit up. And a booster seat (with a safety belt, of course) would be especially nice for travel. They're perfect for restaurants—or when visiting relatives—that don't have their own high chairs. ($20–$50)

❏ Safety gates: Required. Gates need to go at both ends of any staircase, as well as in rooms you don't want baby to have easy access to. You should equip your nest with gates, electric-socket covers, and other precautions to keep baby from doing himself or herself harm. Safety precautions need to be taken care of as soon as baby is in any way mobile. Total baby-proofing costs could run anywhere from $40–$250.

❏ Bouncing seat: Optional—but extremely useful. As soon as baby comes home from the hospital, you will need a quick, safe place to put him down. Our bouncing seat was a godsend. Otherwise, you will end up lugging your carseat in and out of the house. Bouncing seats are more comfortable for baby, too, as they are usually made of cotton instead of the rigid plastic of a carseat. ($20–$40)

❏ Diaper pail: Required. No matter whether you use cloth or disposable diapers, you'll need something to put the dirty ones in. Deciding which to choose will depend on your choice of cloth or disposable. ($10–$35)

Baby Equipment Shopping List

ITEM	MANUFACTURER/PATTERN/COLOR
Bassinet/Cradle	
Crib	
Mattress	
Crib sheets	
Crib liners	
Mobile	
Blanket	
Accessories	
Bumper pads	
Stroller	
Carriage stroller	
Umbrella stroller	
Car seat	
Changing table	
Baby carrier	
Play pen/Porta-Crib	
Rocker	
Baby monitor	

Baby Equipment Shopping List (continued)

ITEM	MANUFACTURER/PATTERN/COLOR
Sling carrier	
Backpack	
High chair	
Booster seat	
Safety gates	
Bouncing seat	
Diaper pail	
General clothing	
Swaddling blanket	
Cloth diapers	
Newborn snap shirt	
Undershirts	
Bunting	
Infant hat	
Sleepers	
Other:	

How Your Baby Grows

About thirteen inches long, your unborn baby is gaining pounds exponentially. He or she may be up to two pounds by the end of this month.

Organs are developed, although the little body is lean with not much sign of fat yet. Sweat glands are forming just beneath the surface of the skin. The face is thin, so the eyes look big and prominent. Eyelids are starting to open and there are eyebrows starting to form. So are the fingernails.

Alternating bursts of activity with periods of rest, your baby experiments with all the amazing movements that can be made with arms and legs. Sit still and concentrate on what may be happening inside. When you sense the moving, kicking, turning, twisting, see if you can detect which part of the fetal body is doing all the pushing and shoving. Is it a foot? An elbow? A head? Or a backside?

He can cough. She can hiccup. Drinking too much of the warm amniotic fluid can bring on these very natural human reactions. Meanwhile, amniotic fluid filled with precious nutrients is excreted from the fetus's body as urine.

Because hearing is becoming even more fine-tuned, the sound of your voice, or certain types of music, are more soothing than ever before.

Frowning, squinting, pursing lips, this little being even has fingerprints now, as well as definite footprints.

What You Can Expect to Experience

Emotional Changes

Inside your rapidly growing belly is a little human being. That you are "in charge" of bringing this fragile treasure into the world can overwhelm you emotionally at times. Flooded with feelings about your baby's safety, the trials of upcoming labor and delivery, and the responsibility of becoming a mother, your moods may swing wildly. It doesn't help, either, when the father-to-be tries to cajole you out of a depressed and cranky state with (what seems to you, at least, to be) a lame joke, such as how easy it is to clean the lint out of your navel. Your ups are higher and your downs are lower now—you never dreamed pregnancy was going to be such a wild ride.

You are not alone. Rest assured, most all mothers-to-be worry. Here are some of the more common concerns of pregnant women:

- Can I be motherly enough?
- What would happen to me after my own baby arrived? Would these instincts really come naturally, or might I fail in the nurturing department?
- What about my future life as an individual? Would I still be able to be a separate person? Or, would I turn into my own mother?
- Unusual, irrational side effects also can establish a place in your mind and refuse to let go. (One woman's ears ached whenever she put on a pair of pierced earrings—even the expensive and hypo-allergenic kinds. Her doctor could find no rational, medical reason for this condition, and the woman was left mystified until a friend admitted she had the same experience; thankfully, after delivery, her ability to wear earrings without ear-ringing, returned to normal.)

Accepting your own tearfulness and fearfulness as natural states can help. Realizing that these concerns are normal and to be expected can help you get through those trying times.

Physical Changes
You're normal if . . .

- You've gained at least ten pounds and your womb has moved well up above your navel.
- Your upper arms seem bigger. Shirts are snug and not just across your bust line. The cause? Probably water retention, not fat.
- Your breasts are still growing and you may need a bigger bra again. (Treat yourself to something lacy or black. Yes, pregnant women can be sexy!)

☆ You are becoming convinced that you may be carrying more than one baby. (Relax. Unless multiple births run in your family, you were taking a fertility drug before you became pregnant, or your doctor and an ultrasound have confirmed the existence of multiple babies, you probably can count on just one little child arriving in about three months.)

☆ You get cramps in your legs and feet especially at night. These cramps plague some women in their legs and can be caused by an imbalance of calcium and phosphorus in your body. Simply increasing the amount of calcium in your diet may not be sufficient, however. According to Dr. Berk, you need aluminum gels or any aluminum-based antacid that will increase the absorption of calcium in a form that will prevent the cramps. Look for Amphi-gel or Rolaids. In the meantime, when a cramp strikes, stretch your leg or point your toes down. If your leg cramp is in the calf, stretch your toes up towards your head. Grab your toes and pull on them. That will stretch the calf muscles out. Of course, it's always great to have a massage. Stand up and walk to the bathroom sink. Wash your hands with warm water; some doctors believe the difference between the warm water on your hands and the cold floor on your bare feet helps to relieve and straighten out the cramp.

☆ Your belly itches. As the skin on your stomach stretches and pulls tighter and tighter, the itchiness may increase. Use a mild skin cream regularly to keep your skin soft and pliable.

☆ You're still breathless and insistent about opening windows everywhere you go.

☆ You experience twinges of pain in your lower abdomen from time to time. Unless you are feeling downright sick, with a fever, congestion, chills, or severe pain, your abdominal sensations are probably just related to stretching liga-

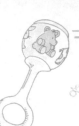

ments and joints. Your uterus is growing rapidly now and causing everything else to be pulled along with it.

⚸ Your lower back still aches. Those muscles and ligaments are so stretched and loosened now that your risk of back injury is high. Your center of gravity is continuing to shift forward, too, which puts a strain on your lower back.

⚸ You've lost your old stamina. The demand on your cardio-vascular system is greater in this second trimester. You may lose steam or energy as a result. Old exercise routines, for instance, aren't quite as easily completed. The urge to quit halfway through is most compelling.

⚸ Your face may be puffy. That's water, too. Speak with your doctor if you are concerned. Regular checkups should be ruling out any serious concerns connected with fluid retention.

The Shape of Things to Come . . .

Just for fun, see if you can put yourself into one of these categories:

⚸ **Are You Carrying a Low-Slung Basketball?**
Your unborn baby won't have to drop at that very last stage of events just before delivery and exit. If this is you, your uterus is still low. In fact, it may not reach up to be tight against your rib cage ever. You could be all out front, causing some strangers to suggest that you are definitely carrying a girl while others insist you are most def-initely having a boy. You may be so low that your waistline is nearly visible and you are tempted to wear a belt some days.

⚸ **Is It a High Ball, However?**
The good news: regular, nonmaternity under-pants may fit fine right until almost the last moment when your baby heads down into the

pelvic area. Unfortunately, your rib cage is gently, but insistently, being pushed up. Get ready for your breasts to rest on your belly, causing a strange, but not necessarily disagreeable, sensation. Unfortunately, you can't wait to take a deep breath.

How About a Watermelon?

If you wanted to recreate the look of this pregnancy after the delivery, you could probably buy a watermelon some summer day and strap it to your waist. Not possible? Of course not. Seriously, your pregnant bulge begins right under your breasts and extends down in a gentle oval to your pubic bone.

Do You Look Like a Pumpkin?

Pumpkin-shaped pregnancies can be emotionally painful because you can appear to be expecting something all over, not just in front. Your growing pumpkin may extend down to the tops of your thighs. A rear-view glance can make you cringe. Don't torture yourself. You will be able to get out of this patch sooner than you think.

What About a Ripened Pear?

Bottom heavy, you may be worrying about your thighs a lot these days because that's where this pregnancy is hitting you hard. No one ever told you that weight gain in pregnancy was not necessarily confined to the abdominal area.

Are You Turning Into a Refrigerator?

Even watching your calories and nutritional needs closely doesn't seem to help reign in this metamorphosis of your body. If you are gaining your weight all over—upper arms, bust, belly, and legs—blame it on a genetic connection. Did your mother put on pregnancy weight in the same way? Relax. Don't accept the grief from the nurses and doctors who refuse to believe you are sticking to a sound diet plan. Yet, don't use the refrigerator shape as an excuse to go wild. After all, you will want to slip back into your old shape in a few months.

Taking Care of Yourself

While many concerns you have during pregnancy won't pan out, there are symptoms that you need to be aware of because they can prove dangerous to your health as well as to your unborn child. You should worry if . . .

♂ **Your Doctor Says That You Are Showing Signs of Preeclampsia**

Also known as *toxemia*, preeclampsia is a complicated, pregnancy-related version of high blood pressure or hypertension, which is more common in first-time mothers-to-be after Week 24. Other signs include: a quick jump in weight gain (from water retention, not baby growth); swollen ankles, feet, or hands; traces of protein in your urine sample; a blood pressure reading of 140/90; a persistent headache; blurry vision; and abdominal pain. Preeclampsia is serious, but treatable. You may end up in bed, either in the hospital or at home. You'll be drinking fluids, watching your sodium or salt intake, and may be put on medication to bring down your high blood pressure. Only a small percentage of pregnant women develop preeclampsia, but it is important for your doctor to keep these symptoms in check before they take you headlong into what is known as eclampsia. If your blood pressure increases to 160/110 or higher, you risk damaging your nervous system, having a seizure, going into a coma, destroying your kidneys and your circulation. Developing a full-blown case, though, is extremely rare for a woman under a doctor's care. However, if your symptoms of preeclampsia remain in your third trimester, labor may be induced or a cesarean section could be recommended. Most women with mild preeclampsia do just fine and blood pressure returns to normal after birth, sometimes within the first day of their baby's life.

You Are Diagnosed with an Incompetent Cervix

Normally in pregnancy, your cervix remains tightly closed until the onset of those first labor pains. If someone is discussing an *incompetent cervix* with you, it means that there is concern about the growing baby and womb putting enough pressure on your weak cervix to open it and cause a miscarriage. Most miscarriages occur in the first trimester, but an incompetent cervix can be cause for concern throughout pregnancy and especially in the second trimester when the baby is not ready to survive. If your cervix has been quietly thinning without any apparent contractions, then the doctor may notice this during an examination. Vaginal bleeding can also be a sign of danger.

An incompetent cervix can be traced back to a number of reasons: a genetic weakness, previous births, prior surgeries, especially abortions, as well as exposure to DES (diethylstilbestrol) when you were in your own mother's womb. If you are carrying more than one baby, you are more likely to have an incompetent cervix, too. Surgery to stitch the cervix tightly closed will be done almost immediately with a diagnosis of incompetency. "It is an emergency," explains Dr. Howard Berk. "If one of my patients walks in and tells me she has a little watery discharge, I'll examine her and if she has an incompetent cervix, she'll be sutured immediately. Then, in any subsequent pregnancy, once this diagnosis of incompetent cervix has been made, the suturing can be done electively about the twelfth to thirteenth week." These sutures will be snipped before your delivery date.

One of the signs of an incompetent cervix is a blood-tinged discharge, so it's important to call your practitioner if this happens in your middle trimester. A test called a *hysterosalpingogram* can indicate an incompetent cervix and will also show adhesions in the womb and tube blockages. The

official name for the suturing surgery is the *Shirodkar procedure*. Other treatments and steps are also available, and you
can be certain that frequent exams will be on your calendar.
Sometimes, bed rest is prescribed, as well as abstinence
from any sexual intercourse. An appliance called a *pessary*,
which is inserted into your vagina, may also be recommended to support the uterus. In the meantime, be certain
to take note of any strange pressure, discharges, or symptoms in your lower abdomen or vagina.

**You Experience a Heavy, "Won't-Go-Away" Pain, Not
a Muscle Cramp, in the Calf of Your Leg**

Unlike ordinary, troublesome cramping, this kind of pain
refuses to disappear within a few minutes. You may see
swelling, redness, and the area could be tender to your
touch. Perhaps the nearby veins look more prominent than
usual. Known as *venous thrombosis*, this condition is a
blood clot that occurs once or twice in every one hundred
pregnancies. You are more likely to develop clots when you
are pregnant. Not only is your body getting ready to stop
any excess flow of blood during birth by strengthening its
clotting ability, but also, because of your enlarged uterus,
blood flow can be impaired and circulation slowed. One of
the symptoms of venous thrombosis is a pain in the area
where you flex or stretch your leg. If the area is tender,
swollen, or you have any other unusual symptoms, don't
wait to seek medical expertise.

You Have Vaginal Bleeding of Any Kind

Bleeding at any time during pregnancy should be reported
to your doctor, but now that you are in your second
trimester, the blood could be a sign of an impending miscarriage, an incompetent cervix, or a problem with the placenta. Occasionally, the placenta has implanted itself close
to, or partially covering, the cervix (*placenta previa*). As
your pregnancy proceeds, this could become the kind of
problem that sends you to the hospital and calls for a

cesarean section at delivery time. An ultrasound can indicate placenta previa. However, even low-lying placentas do move upward as growth continues, so you may simply be sent to bed if your bleeding is light or intermittent. Extra iron, lots of vitamin C, close medical supervision in a hospital setting, and possibly blood transfusions, can keep your baby safe until you reach at least thirty-six weeks in the pregnancy when delivery is safer.

Vaginal bleeding and/or abdominal cramping can also indicate that the placenta has begun to separate from the wall of the uterus, a more serious condition called *placental abruption*. Definitely an emergency, placental abruption survival odds have become better because of good medical care, hospitalization, and early diagnosis. Bed rest has changed the odds of survival dramatically in recent years. Almost all mothers and babies can win this battle beautifully.

RECORD SHEET:
To Our Baby—A Message from Month Six

PHOTO CAPTION: This picture was taken on_____. It shows

_____.

Dear Baby:
Mommy is beginning to look very different. Here's what we've
been doing to get ready for your arrival:

_____
_____
_____
_____
_____
_____
_____
_____
_____

Important Reminders	Scheduled Activities "To Do"

Now is the time to . . .

Monitor your body for any symptoms of potentially serious conditions.
    Talk to your doctor about any of the following conditions, which could be signs of serious trouble:

DAY 1

- High blood pressure or hypertension
- A quick jump in weight gain (from water retention, not baby growth), swollen ankles, feet, or hands
- Traces of protein in your urine sample
- A blood pressure reading of 140/90
- A persistent headache
- Blurry vision
- Abdominal pain
- Bleeding at any time

DAY 2

Schedule/confirm your monthly checkup with your ob/gyn. Record your next regularly scheduled checkup on the appropriate date in this planner!
    Go to the appointment prepared. Continue to track your symptoms. Draft a list of any questions you have. Bring both lists to your next doctor's appointment.
    Schedule regular beauty treatments, such as a haircut, manicure, and pedicure.
    Schedule and plan regular "date nights" with the father-to-be—at least once a week.

DAY 3

Scheduled Activities "To Do"	Important Reminders
	Did you know that . . .

DAY 4

DAY 5

DAY 6

Did you know that . . .

There is no one "right" shape for pregnancy?

Shape Sorting
Some of us carry our unborn babies high, some low, some all over, some hardly at all. (We've all heard those tales of moms wearing their own clothes right into the hospital and then accepting Academy Awards two weeks later while wearing strapless, slinky gowns. Hmmm.) There is little way to predict the physical spin your pregnancy will put on you. This wide variation in pregnancy shaping may not have even dawned on you until now. Most books depend on a single female silhouette to show the shape of things to come. We all know that this pregnant profile is just not true for everyone. In fact, no one knows it more intimately than you do now.

Important Reminders	Scheduled Activities "To Do"

Now is the time to . . .

Shop for footwear.
It's not unusual to go up a full
shoe size during a pregnancy. Your
shoes may feel snug because you
are retaining water in your feet.
The joints in your feet actually do
spread during pregnancy because
the hormone relaxin is loosening
everything up in anticipation of
delivery. That includes feet,
unfortunately. Buy new shoes for
now and think comfort first. Forget
heels. Choose sneakers or walking
shoes. Look for styles that will let
your toes and joints spread out
with ease. Sit down and put your
feet up as often as you can.

DAY 7

DAY 8

DAY 9

DAY 10

....
....
....
....
....
....
....
....
....
....
....
....

DAY 11

....
....
....
....
....
....
....
....
....
....
....
....

DAY 12

....
....
....
....
....
....
....
....
....
....
....
....

*Out of the Mouths of
Mothers . . . and Fathers*

"Your own pregnancy shape is always a surprise when you spot yourself in a mirror or store window. For some reason, I guess because it comes on slowly month by month, you can't easily adjust to that big belly when you look at it squarely. Inside, you are still slim or in the same body you had before."

—A Mom

"Perhaps the strangest thing about the public nature of pregnancy is that many women seem to take it all in stride. I kept waiting for my wife to bite some belly-rubber's hand off, but she never did. For some men, however, this touching business can bring out feelings of anger. 'Nobody touches my woman!'"

—A Dad

Important Reminders	Scheduled Activities "To Do"

Now is the time to . . .

Consider hiring a doula.
A *doula* is a woman who has specialized in helping couples make childbirth a pleasant and productive affair. The word itself is Greek and means "a woman caregiver of another woman." Not exactly midwives, doulas do receive formal training in easing and shortening labor. Some studies do show that working with a doula can change labor significantly, making it shorter by several hours, reducing the likelihood of the need for anesthesia, or of a C-section delivery. If you think you'd like to hire a doula, contact the Doulas of North America, 1100 Twenty-Third Avenue East, Seattle, WA. If your husband is frightened about coaching you through the birth, even after he completes childbirth classes, a doula might be a nice option. As a bonus, a doula also can reach out to the man, decreasing his anxiety, giving him support and encouragement, and allowing him to interact with his partner in a more caring and nurturing way.

DAY 13

DAY 14

DAY 15

Scheduled Activities "To Do"	Important Reminders

DAY 16

DAY 17

DAY 18

Do you know . . .

The high cost of raising a child?
In a report prepared by Philip J. Longman for *U.S. News & World Report*, estimates went as high as $1.45 million for a middle-income family raising a child to age 22. These figures were based on United States Department of Agriculture data which are updated annually. To the federal numbers, however, were added the cost of a college education and the lost wages many mothers experience when they drop out of the job market even for a short while. Higher income families spend as much as $2.78 million, and lower income families spend $761,871 in costs. Longman explains that he didn't even consider the ticket for extras like "soccer camp, cello lessons, and SAT prep."

As for the costs of pregnancy and childbirth, Longman says that a normal, no-risk pregnancy with twelve prenatal visits to the doctor's office and vaginal delivery averages about $2,800 in the U.S. Health insurance turns out to be a financial cost-saver because uninsured expectant moms actually pay more for normal pregnancies and deliveries: $6,400. If you end up with a cesarean section, the bill will be about $11,000 and complicated, high-risk pregnancies go up to $400,000. Every day a premature baby spends in the hospital adds up with a range of $1,000 to $2,500 per diem.

Important Reminders	Scheduled Activities "To Do"

Now is the time to . . .

Assess your priorities.
   A ringing telephone, a doorbell, or the sudden demand of an impatient coworker can make you jump—no matter what else you may have been doing. Even in mid-bite, midsentence, or mid-nap, you may feel obliged to answer all such demands for your time. Urgent requests aren't always important. The next time you start to rush, think: Is this really important, or could it wait?

DAY 19

DAY 20

DAY 21

Scheduled Activities "To Do"	Important Reminders

DAY 22

DAY 23

DAY 24

Important Reminders

Now is the time to . . .

Take advantage of your own biorythms at baby's birth

Now that you have a bit more energy, and you are less fatigued, look for your prime time. There may be twenty-four hours in every day, but your mood and energy level can never keep up around the clock. Some women are at their peak between 10 a.m. and 2 p.m. You know your body best even now. Devote those peak periods to important tasks. Save your mindless routines (or napping) for when you know you'll run out of steam.

Scheduled Activities "To Do"

DAY 25

DAY 26

DAY 27

Scheduled Activities "To Do"	Important Reminders

DAY 28

....
....
....
....
....
....
....
....
....
....
....

DAY 29

....
....
....
....
....
....
....
....
....
....
....

DAY 30/31

....
....
....
....
....
....
....
....
....
....
....
....

Now is the time to . . .

**Check out these
traditional baby décor themes:**

- Animals. Kittens, puppies, teddy bears, and farm scenes are typical within this motif.
- Three-ring circus. Clowns, lions, and tigers can fill baby's room with an exciting array of scenes; and you can create some of your own coordinating pieces—for example, fabric balloon wall hangings.
- Cartoon/TV characters. The advantage to choosing this type of theme is that there are literally hundreds of licensed products that you can purchase.
- Sports teams.
- Noah's Ark. This is a popular theme that transitions well in later childhood.
- Suns, moons, and stars.
- Geometric shapes. These work well in black, red, and white. Many child-development specialists have recommended these contrasting colors for baby's early stimulation and brain development.
- African safari.
- Dolphins, or underwater scenes, with sea-related wall hangings, such as seahorses, sea shells, and waves
- Carousels

Part Three

The
Third
Trimester

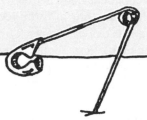

MONTH SEVEN

Planning ahead, You discover more childbirth lingo:
natural, prepared, Lamaze, LeBoyer, LaLeche . . . ,
And personally meet up with Braxton-Hicks.

TO DO THIS MONTH

- ☐ *If you haven't already signed up for childbirth classes, do so now.*

- ☐ *Go over important issues with your doctor.*

- ☐ *Schedule a tour of the hospital or birthing center where you plan to deliver.*

- ☐ *Learn all the signs of premature labor.*

- ☐ *Post emergency phone numbers—your doctor's, for instance—prominently near the kitchen and bedroom phones.*

During the seventh month, you suddenly realize that the baby's delivery and birth are not that far off! You start to feel really confident now that baby is really on the way. Until now, you may have felt torn in two directions: Looking towards the future, reading catalogs of nursery furniture and baby clothes, but with a nagging uneasiness about buying things for someone who has not yet entered the world. If you were holding back a little on decorating the nursery or preparing for labor and delivery, this is the month when you realize you had better get moving. There's tons of stuff to do before the baby arrives . . . and less time than ever to do it in!

Take a deep breath, gather your thoughts, and proceed in a logical fashion (granted, that's not too easy during this emotional phase of your life). Focus especially on learning relaxation and breathing techniques for delivery. The sooner you start practicing them, the better. By the time you're in the delivery room or birthing suite, you want these techniques to be second nature to you. It's also important to think about what you believe would really help things go more smoothly. No book can tell you what would really make you rise to the childbearing challenge with ease, but here are some things to try:

- Give some thought to what would make the birthing process and after birth experience less stressful for you. Could things at home be better organized? Would it help to have a housecleaner, nanny, or someone to help with the cooking for a few weeks? Make a list, and start trying to organize solutions.
- Investigate massage. Some massage therapists specialize in childbirth, and can help enhance the experience for both mother and child.
- Resolve questions about labor, delivery, life with a newborn, and any other issues with your doctor and healthcare providers.
- Pick out some music to give birth to . . . choose a piece of music to practice controlled breathing to. Start playing it now so that by the time you go to the hospital, listening to it will have an automatically de-stressing effect on you. The same

song can be a piece of music especially chosen to welcome your baby into the world. A family member of mine chose "It's a Wonderful World." She played it every day during her pregnancy (yes, the fetus *can* hear), and, when her newborn baby got fussy, she would play it again, and it more often than not would soothe her daughter.

♂ Post emergency phone numbers—your doctor's, for instance—prominently near the kitchen and bedroom phones.

This Month's Priorities

❑ If you haven't already signed up for childbirth classes, do so now.
❑ Go over important issues with your doctor.
❑ Schedule a tour of the hospital or birthing center where you plan to deliver.
❑ Learn all the signs of premature labor.

Childbirth Classes

Learning the Lingo

Lamaze

Named after a French doctor, Fernand Lamaze, Lamaze classes are among the most popular classes in the United States today and can be taken privately, or in a hospital. Set breathing exercises are stressed for each stage of labor, as are important relaxation techniques. Also emphasized to take your mind off your labor pains is the need to focus on something, almost hypnotically: a poster, your husband's face, a speck on the wall.

Dick-Read

Based on a British doctor's theories, these classes emphasize slow abdominal breathing and teach you how to focus on the feelings and signals your own body sends during labor.

Bradley

Denver obstetrician Robert Bradley developed this approach about fifty years ago, and childbirth people call it the "no-method" method. It's closer to Dick-Read than to Lamaze in theory. Classes teach couples how to relax and breathe deeply, but emphasis is on doing what comes naturally—having the presence of dads-to-be, proper nutrition during pregnancy, and, most importantly, knowing all the options beforehand.

LeBoyer

To soften what he called the harsh trauma of being born, this French doctor advocated low lights in the delivery room, a warm bath for the new baby, calm voices, and soothing room temperatures. Some American physicians thought he was crazy back in the 1970s.

Class Ingredients: What Makes a Good One Good for You

If you've been feeling swamped by life lately, you may wonder why you need to take a class at all. Seriously, when your life is already busy and you are anticipating a time in your future when the concept of personal space disappears almost entirely, do you need to go out at night, commune with strangers, and listen to an expert describing a biological process that may be frightening you? Yes, of course.

The Ins, Outs, Ups and Downs of Childbirth Classes

Even if your library of reading material about pregnancy, labor, and the birth process is already overflowing, there is nothing more worthwhile than taking a class to prepare you and your mate for what lies ahead. Honestly, reading about pregnancy just isn't enough. Here is what to expect:

- You will sit in a class, side-by-side with other pregnant couples near your own stage of development, and drink in the emotional and physical support that can come from sharing experiences.
- You will listen to a trained childbirth educator, who can offer support and information. You may find yourself asking questions you wouldn't dare bring up with your doctor.
- You will discuss all kinds of nitty-gritty details and fears with other couples forging ahead into the same great unknown as yourself. Even scary or weird dreams aren't off limits when you are among the instant friends you find in childbirth classes.
- You'll get detailed descriptions of the birth process. Sure, you skipped ahead to sections on labor and delivery and think you may know more than enough, but you don't. Aspects of childbirth that seem pretty clear on paper will become even more understandable and predictable when you are in a good class that suits you and your general approach to the kind of birth you'd like to have.
- You can pick up even more details about your hospital or birthing center.
- You learn the best coping strategies, including how to breathe, relaxation techniques, all about anesthesia or other pain-controlling methods, and what each stage of labor will demand of your body and your mind.
- Your partner will learn how to offer you comfort. Classes, in fact, are especially important for fathers-to-be because they take the unknown out of the fear.
- You will learn to take one step at a time during labor and delivery because you will understand that those waves of contractions ebb and flow and certainly have a finish line with a happy ending.

Choosing a Teacher

Although not all childbirth preparation classes are created equal, most will offer you a wonderful opportunity to learn, and by learning as much as you can, you'll be less fearful and may end up having less pain. Some courses are intense, begin early in pregnancy, and try to take you through the whole nine months. Most hospital-based programs feature eight weekly sessions that start somewhere in the last trimester and are taught by a hospital employee who may spend quite a bit of time emphasizing in-house practices and procedures. Other classes are designed to be simple, one-night refresher courses for couples who simply want to brush up on ideas and techniques they learned for previous births. You may even want to sign up for baby CPR or safety classes, which will take you through all the emergency and first aid steps for your baby after birth. These classes aren't designed to scare you, but to prepare you. Don't miss this chance to start life as a mother fully prepared for the best, the worst, and all the in-between.

Do some thought work and homework first. Think about how you feel about being in pain, and whether you will want to be given medication. If you are certain you will want to have an epidural, a type of anesthesia administered directly into the spaces between the vertebrae of your spine, you don't want to find yourself listening to an instructor who believes in an all-natural, no-drugs approach to birth. Your hospital may be the most natural route to a good class, and possibly the cheapest. Call to find out when, where, and what kind of philosophy, if any, the educator espouses. Childbirth or Midwifery Centers offer classes. Ask your doctor or his staff for recommendations. If you want to find a private class that may also be less crowded than the hospital route, you can call the International Childbirth Education Association (ICEA) at (612) 854-8660 for the names of certified instructors in your area. According to information offered on their Web site (http://www.icea.org), ICEA "is a professional organization that supports educators, parents, and other health-care providers who believe in knowledge and freedom of choice in family-centered maternity and newborn care." Classes taught by an ICEA-trained educator, "typically focus on using as little medical inter-

vention as possible but will provide you with an overview of all your options." For more information about ICEA, write P.O. Box 20048, Minneapolis, MN 55420.

Types of Childbirth

Natural

An award for the most-asked question must go to: "Will you be having natural childbirth?" By all rights, "natural" should mean nothing—no classes, no drugs, no hospital, no preparation. However, in most of today's birth literature, this term has come to mean an awake, aware, undrugged mother. It does not mean, as some people believe, a painless birth. (In childbirth, some women have a lot of pain and some have almost none.) Many women wrongly feel they've failed if they can't stand the pain and need a sedative.

Prepared

The best general word encompassing all the childbirth classes today is *prepared childbirth*, which can include lectures, exercise instructions, tours of maternity/obstetrics departments, and may combine several theories on how to manage labor.

Lamaze

If it's a Lamaze class, named after the French doctor Fernand Lamaze, you will learn how to manage your pain using relaxation exercises and deep-breathing techniques. Dr. Lamaze, whose book *Painless Childbirth* was published in 1956, believes that all laboring women must have "a thorough preparation given by qualified people and a guarantee of peace, silence, comfort and the help of a qualified assistant during the whole of the labor." First witnessed by the doctor during a summer trip to Russia in 1951, the basis of Lamaze's work springs from a researcher named Ivan Pavlov, who believed that repetition and training could change thought processes.

With thirty years of experience as an obstetrician back in France, Lamaze was amazed to see women in Russia giving birth with virtually no pain because they had learned a practiced response, or a reflexive action, to use during labor and delivery. By concentrating intensely on a particular stimulus or action, you are supposed to be able to diminish your physical feelings. Let's call it mind over matter, and yes, it does work for some women, some of the time.

Lamaze took the Russian ideas and taught his French patients a series of respiratory responses: slow breathing during the first stage of labor, rapid breathing during the second stage, and a panting type of breathing as the child's head presents itself. His rather famous approach is called *psychoprophylaxis*.

If you sign up for an Americanized, updated version of a Lamaze course, the ICEA says you'll probably have twelve hours of instruction, be asked to bring your pillow for getting comfortable during practice sessions, and learn all about staying as pain-free as possible during the birth. However, Lamaze won't frighten you away from using anesthesia if this is a choice you find you must make. You'll get background information on epidurals and other anesthesias. More than two million parents choose a Lamaze childbirth class. For more information about the American Society of Psychoprophylaxis in Obstetrics (the official name for the Lamaze method), call 1-800-368-4404. You can also find them on the computer at their Web site, *http://lamaze-childbirth.com*.

Bradley-Based Coaching

Another well-known approach to childbirth education is the Bradley method, which was actually the first to introduce the idea of husbands acting as coaches. Bradley's ideas are built on education, breathing, relaxation, and a husband-coach. If you find yourself speaking with a Bradley teacher, you should know that these educators always go through a regular recertification process, which is good news for you because they will be up-to-date on the latest in medicine and obstetrical circles. They will also emphasize the importance of a healthy diet and regular exercise. However, Bradley instructors try to ease you through the process with as little medication as possible, so if you've decided you want to leave your options open about anesthesia, you may want to reconsider a Bradley-based class.

Grantly Dick-Read

Another childbirth preparation crusader whose name you may encounter in your search of theories is Dr. Grantly Dick-Read, a British obstetrician who was determined to change the way women experienced so much pain during the birth process. His first book, *Natural Childbirth*, was published in England in 1933. Dr. Dick-Read believed that knowledge was power and got himself in so much trouble sharing his wisdom about labor, delivery, and other obstetrical intricacies that he was actually shunned by the British Medical Society, as well as the Anglican Church. He suspected that fear overstimulated the central nervous system and compounded whatever normal, natural pains a woman might be having during labor. Get rid of the fear and you may just be able to get rid of the pain. When he died, an obituary in the *British Journal of Obstetrics and Gynecology* called him "a crusader with almost too much fire in his belly," explains Dr. Elizabeth Whelan in *The Pregnancy Experience*. If you can get your hands on old books, you might also find it interesting to browse through Dick-Read's other works: *Childbirth without Fear, Natural Childbirth Primer,* and *Introduction to Motherhood*.

The Bing Option

People in childbirth circles consider Elisabeth Bing, who has based her ideas on Dr. Lamaze's thinking, to be a leader in her approach to the use of psychoprophylaxis. Her book, *Six Practical Lessons for an Easier Childbirth*, is a classic, and she's known for her no-guilt, no-nonsense style. "You will learn to change your breathing deliberately during labor, adjusting it to the changing characteristics of the uterine contractions. This will demand an enormous concentrated effort on your part. Not a concentration on pain, but a concentration on your own activity in synchronizing your respiration to the signals that you receive from the uterus," she explains. "This strenuous activity will create a new center of concentration in the brain, thereby causing painful sensations during labor to become peripheral, to reduce their intensity."

Questions to Ask a Childbirth Instructor

Ask these suggested questions:

1. Where did you get your teacher training?
   _____
   _____

2. How long have you been teaching?
   _____
   _____

3. Have you given birth using this method?
   _____
   _____

4. Where do you hold classes? How often does your class meet?
   _____
   _____

5. How big are your classes?
   _____
   _____

6. Can I call you with questions between classes?
   _____
   _____

7. How much does a class cost?
   _____
   _____

8. Can you recommend couples I can call for references?

   Name _____ Phone _____

   Name _____ Phone _____

   Name _____ Phone _____

9. Do your classes cover:

   Exercises and conditioning?

   _____

   Nutritional information?

   _____

   Relaxation techniques?

   _____

   Preparation for the labor coach?

   _____

   Breastfeeding instruction?

   _____

   Newborn care?

   _____

10. What are your thoughts on taking drugs for pain relief during labor?

    _____

    _____

    _____

    _____

    _____

    _____

    _____

Review Important Issues with Your Doctor

Mothers-to-be sometimes feel as if they have no say in the childbirth process, with all of the policies hospitals and medical institutions have. Even though many institutions have come to agree that, whenever medically possible, the feelings of mothers, babies, and fathers should come first, and hospital policies second, you may be in for a surprise when the moment of delivery comes. You thought your sister or best friend and your husband could be present, but the hospital says no. You thought your baby would stay in your room, but the hospital says no. What's important for you to realize is that you do have choices. Before you go to your regular checkup this month, be sure to make a list of your concerns and questions. Don't assume that you understand exactly what your doctor is planning or how the hospital works. Think about your expectations for delivery—down to every last detail. Then review your view of things with your doctor. Don't feel like any point you need to cover is too small or insignificant. Ask.

Scheduling a Tour of the Hospital Delivery Room or Birthing Center

Birthing Options

Hospital Birth

Let's face it, hospitals can offer you all the equipment and the experts you may need. Drugs for pain medication, electronic fetal monitoring machines to track the progress of your labor and the baby inside, and everything for emergency intervention will be right at your bedside, or at least nearby. A couple of days' rest afterward in a clean, comfortable bed where you will be fed and comforted by nurses is also an option most women go for. While many hospitals try to hurry you out as quickly as possible after a normal delivery, you may be able to stretch your stay up to forty-eight hours. Ask for information about what your insurance plan provides. First-time mothers also welcome the inside information, hands-on care, and nurturing that are often available from obstetrical and pediatric nurses.

Take the Tour

Even if this is the very same hospital where you've visited all your recuperating relatives for years, and you know the gift shop wares by heart, don't skip the tour of the obstetric and maternity areas. You will quickly find out about family-centered activities, including visiting hours or policies for husbands and siblings. Word-of-mouth tips are worth seeking, so ask other moms who have delivered at your hospital of choice.

Birthing Rooms

If you deliver in a typical hospital setting, you will labor in one room, and just before the baby is ready to be born, you will be transferred down the hall to the delivery room or operating room. All this movement can come at a most inopportune time. There can be no worse feeling for a mom who has been in labor for many hours and who is ready to  push out her baby than to be told, "Hold on a minute. We need to transfer you to the delivery room." In recent years, more hospitals have realized that moving a woman so close to delivery is not a very nice thing to do. Birthing rooms within the hospital setting are designed for low-risk pregnancies, and if you and your doctor expect things to go normally, then ask for a reservation. You'll stay in one spot from beginning to end, and these rooms usually offer homey touches. Find out if the room has a birthing bed or one with a split frame, so that a bottom portion of the bed can detach at the time of delivery. It may be more comfortable for you, and the doctor or midwife can simply pull up a chair to help ease your baby out into the light of day. If you think you would prefer this option, speak up early so your name will be added to the list.

Birthing Centers

Small, out-of-hospital facilities, these centers may be an option if you are in a normal, low-risk category. Occasionally, hospitals actually operate them on their own grounds or nearby. Sometimes staffed by midwives and obstetricians on call for emergencies, birthing centers can also provide your regular prenatal checkups, childbirth classes, and some routine testing. If you are interested in learning more about birthing centers near you, contact the American College of Nurse-Midwives, 1522 K Street, NW, Suite 1000, Washington, DC 20005.

Home Births

Some healthy, expectant mothers prefer to stay right at home during childbirth. If this is a path on your wish list, do make sure to plan ahead carefully. You need an expert—an obstetrician, experienced family doctor, a competent nurse-midwife—to remain with you during your labor and delivery. You can't do this alone or with the single-handed assistance of your partner. Arranging a home birth is possible, but you may have to dig for resources and information. If you know of a mother who has successfully remained relaxed amidst her own family and familiar comfort zone for the birth of her baby, then ask about her arrangements and who handled the birth.

A home birth is not a good idea if you have any kind of long-standing health condition, including diabetes, heart or kidney disorder, a history of problems in childbirth, previous C-section, or if you go into labor prematurely. If you smoke or are carrying more than one baby, consider a hospital your safest bet, too.

Premature Labor

Having a baby between the twentieth and thirty-seventh week of pregnancy is considered premature. Preemies can suffer from a wide range of neurological and physical difficulties and may simply be too undeveloped to survive at all. Stories of miracle babies surviving after spending only 20 weeks inside their mothers' warm, nurturing womb can make you cry with delight. However, even with all the advances in neonatology, you really want to avoid delivering before your term is up. In this, as well as in so many aspects of life, timing is everything. Most pregnancies depend on a delicate hormonal, biochemical phenomenon that will allow labor to begin safely after the thirty-seventh week. Every effort to keep your baby safely inside will be made when premature contractions threaten to end your pregnancy too soon.

At the first inkling of any signs of impending labor, some practitioners will tell you to lie down, rest slightly on your side, and put a pillow along your back for support. Don't turn completely sideways because you may not be able to feel the contractions as definitively. Keep timing the contractions, noting the actual time on the clock at the beginning as well as the end.

Premature labor will call for quick action on your part as well as your doctor's. Some doctors believe in a regimen of complete bed rest as well as drugs to relax your uterus from contracting. You could also end up in the hospital. Even if you remain home, you will be closely monitored. Drugs designed to stop contractions and slow up your baby's arrival are controversial and can have side effects. However, if the cervix is starting to dilate and the uterus is contracting, you may only delay the event a little by going to bed, by raising your feet and relying on gravity, and by having a pessary (an instrument put into the vagina to support the uterus) inserted.

Not all cases of premature labor result in a preterm birth. Although you may not really know exactly what triggered your early labor, if your contractions stop, your womb remains a healthy place for your baby to stay, no amniotic fluid has leaked, and your cervix is tightly closed, your pregnancy could proceed without further interruption. However, if your cervix softens, or effaces, and opens to more than four or five centimeters, early birth may be unavoidable. Rest assured that a very small percentage of babies are born prematurely, and with the advances in neonatology and obstetrical care, survival rates have increased dramatically. A regional network of perinatal care for premature infants, staffed by experts trained in the care of newborns at risk, is available to better your baby's chances of living happily ever after. Because operating these units is so expensive, not all hospitals offer this very special baby care with state-of-the-art maternal and fetal medicine. Hospitals fall into three categories as far as preemies' care is concerned: Level III, II, and I.

Level II hospitals can care for normal pregnancies and some high-risk cases. Sometimes, level II hospitals work closely with level IIIs on a consultation basis. If your hospital has a level I classification, it just isn't equipped to care for you on a long-term basis if you or your baby encounter special difficulties.

You are at risk for premature, or preterm labor if

- you have already had a baby prematurely
- you are carrying more than one baby now
- your cervix has been deemed incompetent
- you have had a series of infections in your urinary tract or cervical area
- your uterus is abnormal in any way
- you have had an abortion before
- you are under eighteen or over forty
- you are obese
- you are too thin and trying to stay that way for some misguided reason
- you develop a fever with a really high temperature
- you had surgery on your uterus
- you have high blood pressure
- you develop a kidney, liver, or heart problem
- you are severely anemic
- you are exercising much too strenuously
- you are a heavy smoker
- you are drinking alcohol or using drugs
- you suffer a severe emotional breakdown
- your mother took DES*

* (DES stands for diethylstilbestrol and was once pre-scribed to women with obstetrical problems, diabetes, or vaginal bleeding during pregnancy. DES turned out to cause major problems for the daughters of women who were prescribed DES because it caused abnormal changes in their cervixes and/or vaginas. If you were exposed to DES in utero, then your practitioner will automatically place you in the high-risk category

Good Idea: Ask Your Doctor About the Closest Level III Hospital. A Level III Neonatal Care Hospital will feature:

- ❏ Capability of managing even the most complicated, high-risk births
- ❏ Transport, even by air, of the mother and baby to its facility or another hospital in its network. (You could end up in a helicopter, and these medical centers have heliports.)
- ❏ Every kind of testing imaginable.
- ❏ Fetal monitoring equipment
- ❏ Sophisticated surgical procedures even for the tiniest baby
- ❏ Amniocentesis
- ❏ Diagnostic ultrasound
- ❏ Genetic studies and counseling
- ❏ Special laboratory and pathology testing
- ❏ Neonatal intensive care units
- ❏ Educational programs for you as the new mom
- ❏ Special programs for expectant moms who are known to be at high risk because of a preexisting health disorder such as diabetes, heart disease, or epilepsy
- ❏ A team of very skilled professionals at your service

How Your Baby Grows

Your unborn baby has reached a landmark in development by this seventh month. Chances of survival outside your body get better and better now, day-by-day. Your baby is getting close to four pounds in weight and sixteen inches in length. These gains in size will be phenomenal during this last trimester.

The top of your uterus is halfway between your belly button and your breastbone, and it is cramping all your internal organs, especially your stomach, intestines, and diaphragm.

Beneath red, wrinkled skin, fat is accumulating, which makes your baby appear flesh-colored. The lanugo, a downy covering of hair, is shedding, and real hair on the head will soon start growing. Dramatic developments in the thinking part of the brain take place this month. A seven-month-old fetus feels pain, can cry, and behaves almost like a full-term infant. When stimulated by light or sound, your fetus will respond. Eyes are open with real eyebrows and eyelashes, too.

Your ability to feel all the activities inside depend on your build, the position of your placenta, and the baby's size. Have your mate place his hands gently up against your abdomen during the early evening hours, or when you suspect the baby is likely to be up and about. Sometimes the baby will react to the sense of touch from your outside world.

Your unborn baby has a strong sense of taste, and some experts suspect that fetal taste buds are actually stronger in the womb than after birth. Missing a critical ingredient known as *surfactant*, the lungs wouldn't be quite operable in the real world yet. Surfactant keeps them from collapsing in between breaths. Yet, surfactant can be increased in the fetus by giving intramuscular steroids to the mother prior to her delivery. Also, when membranes rupture, or other forms of stress occur, surfactant increases. Chemical surfactants can be used after birth to help with respiratory distress. That slight, repetitive jarring you sense could be hiccups, which have been known to continue for up to a half-hour.

What You Can Expect to Experience

Emotional Changes

The language spoken by people in the childbirth community is dotted with a curious mixture of medicalese, French, and European imports with a sociological/psychological flavor. If you haven't been pregnant before or close to someone who has been, some of the terms may be puzzling. You may feel intimidated this month. Don't be. If you have a question, ask for an answer, no matter how silly you think it sounds or how professionally officious the expert—nurse, doctor, midwife, resident, intern, neonatologist—in front of you appears to be. Some questions have already been answered and issues settled by this seventh month. Yet, a refresher on the basics is always nice to have on hand.

You don't pass or fail childbirth classes, so relax. There are no As, Bs, or Fs at the end of this term of instruction. Your goal is to learn as much as you can about childbirth and how to relax during the entire experience. If this is your first birth, you really don't know how your labor and delivery will feel, but let's face it, the odds and research indicate that you are going to have at least some discomfort. The expectant moms who are prepared are able to deal with it better. Even if you have some preconceived notion that you won't need anesthesia, you can always change your mind with no guilt. Seriously, rehearsing your approach to each stage of labor helps. Taking childbirth classes can shorten the length of your labor.

Physical Changes
You're normal if . . .

- *You have heartburn and gassy, bloated constipation.* Eat small meals if your appetite is large but your stomach is resisting. Skip the greasy fries and spicy foods. You'll feel better without indigestion. Eat as many fruits and vegetables as you can stand to ease constipation. Don't rely on laxatives, especially the ones that contain a compound called *phenolphthalein*. Along with your fruits and veggies, go with bran cereals, prune juice, and lots of water every day. Don't lie down right after eating because the uterus pressing on a full stomach can make you incredibly uncomfortable.
- *Getting out of bed is getting difficult.* While you have been trying out new sleeping positions in your efforts to get comfortable at night, a new sensation could be your inability to get up eas-

ily. Roll to your side and then push up with your hands. Don't try to sit up suddenly and put your feet quickly on the floor.

You have swollen ankles and fingers. Called *edema*, this condition happens to almost everyone during this last trimester. Your body is holding on to extra water. Have you noticed swelling in your ankles, especially during hot weather or at the end of the day? Show your practitioner, but don't worry. If your rings don't fit your fingers easily now, that's to be expected, too. However, keep in mind that dramatic swelling could be a sign of preeclampsia.

Your skin is extra sensitive and prone to a pimplelike condition featuring little red bumps on your stomach, thighs, and/or backside. Your face can also break out in a bevy of blemishes and prominent pimples. Hormonal changes are partially to blame, but so is the tension building up now. Breakouts, rashes, allergic reactions, extreme oiliness, and patches of flaky dryness are part of the pregnancy picture. Don't be alarmed. Bring up your dermatological concerns at your next office visit. Ask about creams, lotions, cleansing routines, and makeup.

You have back pain. If the pain in your lower back or buttocks is also sending its message down the back of your leg, you may have *sciatica*, or a swelling of one of the discs in your spine. The sciatic nerve could actually be pinched. The joints in your lower back are not functioning happily together because your growing uterus is forcing you into awkward positions. If you don't remember lifting, bending suddenly while trying to turn your body, or doing anything that might have brought on your pain, your dramatically changing posture could be the cause. Sometimes sciatica disappears when the baby changes positions. Ask your doctor about analgesics or safe drugs to reduce the inflammation. Put a heating pad on your pain. Inquire about special exercises.

You aren't comfortable resting when you lie on your back. If you try to rest on your back during the last trimester, your enlarged uterus falls back and may decrease some blood flow to your heart. As a result, your blood pressure drops. You can't get comfortable. Lie on your left side and your circulatory system can work better.

❋ *Your breasts are leaking and still growing bigger.* Not only are your breasts heavier, but also they are more glandular and getting ready to feed your baby. In this last trimester, they may begin to leak colostrum, which is the nutrient-rich fluid that precedes real breast milk. Estrogen and proges- terone are reaching record high levels in your system and orchestrating all kinds of pregnancy-related changes.

Your breasts may also need a lot of support, so look for a bra that has extra wide straps. If you are wearing a D cup or larger, this strap width makes good sense. Find a style that will cover your entire breast with a full underarm and inner- cup support system. Some designs actually have soft-stretch elastic let-out darts in the front that can grow with you during these last months of pregnancy. If your breasts are really big, bend over when you fasten your bra to allow your breasts to fall into the cups' natural positions. You'll get a better fit. Also, make sure that the bra is snug around your chest. If it is too loose, it will ride up your back and push your breasts forward and down. If you are planning to breastfeed, con- sider buying your nursing bras now. Some can be adjusted for size easily.

❋ *You may experience Braxton-Hicks contrac- tions, or false labor pains.* Out of nowhere, you'll feel the tightening grip of the muscles surrounding your baby. Then, quickly, there is a gradual release. These Braxton-Hicks contractions can start happening after Week 20, continuing right up until your due date when the real act of birth begins. A big difference

between a Braxton-Hicks and a real labor pain is that the cervix remains closed tightly. Consider these belly-tightening and cramping sensations a warm-up for the real labor yet to come; and in fact, they do seem to be nature's way of getting those muscles in your uterus ready for labor and delivery. For a few seconds, you may actually see your uterus harden, a strange sensation that can last as long as two minutes. Nearly painless and unlike real labor contractions, which have a predictable pattern and timing, the Braxton-Hicks variety are irregular and can hit you anywhere, anytime. If you are uncomfortable during a Braxton-Hicks, try changing positions. Sit down. Lie down. Stand up. In a swimming pool? Climb out and sit in the sun for a minute.

To check your unexpected contractions, lie down and put your fingertips on each side of your uterus. You may be able to feel the contractions better in this position. Keep still for a half-hour. Sometimes, the uterus contracts so painlessly that you can't feel it when you are up and running around. Some experts recommend that all expectant moms who are in a high-risk category check for contractions in this way regularly. If you've experienced any bleeding since your fifth month, put this practice into your daily routine. You just don't want your baby's early arrival to catch you off guard.

Starting at the twentieth week, the uterus has a basic rhythm. The smooth muscle of the uterus is similar to your intestinal tract or the heart. All have peristalsis, or wavelike contractions, so painless contractions are not labor. Painful contractions are labor. The actual definition of labor, even when it is premature, is the onset of painful, uterine contractions that lead to a change in the cervix and end with the delivery of the baby.

Taking Care of Yourself

Fourteen Mother-Friendly Pointers

1. Make your pregnancy as stress-free as possible. *Pssst. Don't*

tackle anything new. Don't plan elaborate parties, vacations, or encounters with difficult people. Pamper yourself. You are not being selfish. You are taking good care of your baby.

2. Keep your doctor and medical team informed about any change of side effects or strange sensations.

3. Put emergency phone numbers and names in prominent places. Post them next to your kitchen phone. Carry them with you in your pocketbook.

4. Don't worry about appearing to be dubbed a nervous nilly by your doctor or nurses. You want to make sure that your body remains the warm, welcoming, nurturing environment it has been for the last six months because your baby needs to stay there as long as possible.

5. Build an at-home library of resource materials, including books, pamphlets, Web sites, and other moms' notes. Store your paperwork in one place so you can retrieve it when you need to research some particular side effect or funny feeling.

6. Don't keep your worries to yourself. Share your fears with your mate.

7. Skip strenuous exercise. You will get your body back soon enough.

8. Don't worry about getting all your chores done every day.

9. Think about taking an early leave of absence from your job if you are still employed away from home. Get a note from your doctor if you are worried about reactions at work.

10. Don't try to decorate the baby's room by yourself.

11. Stop lifting grocery bags and heavy objects.

12. Don't expect to shop non-stop unless you are browsing through catalogs.

13. Put your feet up and sit still every day as often and for as long as you can.

14. Be sure to discuss your sex life during regular office visits because the doctor may want you to abstain from intercourse until after the baby is born. Some physicians actually issue a no-sex warning after the fifth month for expectant moms in high-risk categories for premature labor.

RECORD SHEET:
To Our Baby—A Message from Month Seven

Photo Caption: This picture was taken on_____. It shows

_____.

Dear Baby:
The funniest things happen in childbirth classes. We learned:

_____
_____
_____
_____
_____
_____
_____
_____

Important Reminders

Now is the time to . . .

- **Schedule/confirm your check-up with your ob/gyn.** Record your next regularly scheduled checkup on the appropriate date in this planner!
- **Go to the appointment prepared.** Continue to track your symptoms. Draft a list of any questions you have. Bring both lists to your next doctor's appointment.
- **Continue taking vitamins.**
- **Read about labor and delivery.**
- **Put emergency phone numbers and names in prominent places. Post them next to your kitchen phone. Carry them with you in your pocketbook.**

Scheduled Activities "To Do"

DAY 1

DAY 2

DAY 3

Scheduled Activities "To Do"	Important Reminders

DAY 4

DAY 5

DAY 6

Now is the time to . . .

Learn the difference between real and false labor.
Real labor has a rhythm with contractions that occur very regularly and grow stronger and more frequent. If you are really going into labor early, you will be able to time the length of each contraction, as well as the calm interval in between this tightening or hardening of your uterus. You'll find a pattern. It could be one every ten minutes, one every twenty minutes, or one every hour. Pick up a pad and pencil and keep track if you suspect that a contraction could be the start of something more serious. Write down the exact time, how long the contraction lasts, and when the next one occurs. Time yourself for at least an hour. More than five within sixty minutes should send you to the telephone to alert your practitioner.

Important Reminders	Scheduled Activities "To Do"

Did you know that . . .

- The top of your uterus is halfway between your belly button and breastbone by now?
- Half of all pregnant women have back pain?
- By lying on your left side, your circulation will work better and sleeping soundly will be easier?
- If your baby arrives prematurely, you both may be sent to the nearest "Level III" hospital, i.e., one with a neonatal intensive care unit?

DAY 7

DAY 8

DAY 9

Scheduled Activities "To Do"	Important Reminders

DAY 10

....
....
....
....
....
....
....
....
....
....

DAY 11

....
....
....
....
....
....
....
....
....
....
....

DAY 12

....
....
....
....
....
....
....
....
....
....

Now is the time to . . .

Rest easier at night.

"When I have a patient who is markedly edematous—retaining an excess amount of fluid—or who has hypertension, I suggest that she lie on her left side from twelve to one during the day. The purpose of this timing is to decrease the production of a hormone called aldosterone, which regulates your electrolytes. This hormone is excreted when you lie on your back, sit, or stand, but never when you lie on your side. Aldosterone is also not excreted at night. Have you ever noticed that you weigh less in the morning than when you went to bed the night before? The reason is that you have turned off your production of aldosterone and have breathed your water out. If you have excess fluid in your body, lying on your left side at noontime will make you rest easier at night."
—Dr. Howard Berk

Now is the time to . . .

Get Help Right Away if You have These Signs of Premature Labor

- Painful contractions every ten minutes or even more often.
- Cramps in your lower abdomen that remind you of menstrual pains.
- Pressure just above your pubic bone.
- Stomach pain.
- Backache at the bottom of your spinal cord. (This is a dull pain that's different from any other backaches you've had during pregnancy so far.)
- A change in your vaginal discharge. (You probably recognize the sticky, white leukorrhea by now. In premature labor, you could be leaking mucus that is watery or slightly bloody.)
- Blood stains on your underpants any time from the fifth to the ninth month.

DAY 13

DAY 14

DAY 15

Scheduled Activities "To Do"	Important Reminders

DAY 16

....
....
....
....
....
....
....
....
....
....

DAY 17

....
....
....
....
....
....
....
....
....
....

DAY 18

....
....
....
....
....
....
....
....
....
....

Now is the time to . . .

Review your symptoms.
In your seventh month, it's normal to experience:

- Tender, growing breasts that may leak sticky colostrum
- Lack of stamina
- Achy, swollen feet and puffy ankles, face, and hands
- Backaches
- Breathlessness, lightheadedness
- Frequent urination
- Insomnia
- Constipation, indigestion, heartburn, and stomach, as well as intestinal, gas
- Hemorrhoids
- Runny nose, stuffy sinuses
- Headaches
- Vaginal discharges
- Stretch marks and varicose veins
- Skin flareups and hair hassles
- Braxton-Hicks contractions
- Fetal movements

Now is the time to . . .

Learn how to say NO.

Turning down someone who asks for a chunk of your time is never simple, but these suggestions may help:

- Say it fast before they can anticipate a yes. Hedging with "I don't know" or "Let me think about it" only complicates your life now, adding stress when you may want to excuse yourself later.
- Be polite and pleasant.
- Offer a counterproposal.

DAY 19

DAY 20

DAY 21

Scheduled Activities "To Do"	Important Reminders

Now is the time to . . .

Contact your local chapter of La Leche League International if you are interested in breastfeeding.
La Leche is a Spanish phrase meaning "the milk." This organization was founded in the 1950s to promote breastfeeding in the United States when the practice was at an all time low. It offers local groups and books that provide information, as well as emotional support, for women who wish to breastfeed.

DAY 22

DAY 23

DAY 24

Important Reminders	Scheduled Activities "To Do"

Did you know that . . .

When it comes to newborn care, hospitals fall into three categories?
Find out if your hospital is Level III, II, or I. Level II hospitals can care for normal pregnancies and some high-risk cases. Sometimes, level II hospitals work closely with level IIIs on a consultation basis. If your hospital has a level I classification, it just isn't equipped to care for you on a long-term basis if you or your baby encounter special difficulties.

DAY 25

DAY 26

DAY 27

Scheduled Activities "To Do"	Important Reminders

DAY 28

DAY 29

DAY 30/31

Now is the time to . . .

Make some decisions.
If all goes well and you reach your ninth month safely, soundly, and still pregnant, the choices you make regarding classes, labor, delivery, and birth will affect you, your baby, and the way you begin your lives together. Don't duck these issues by allowing other people to make your decisions.

- Will it be Lamaze, LeBoyer, natural, prepared, medicated, or wide awake?
- Will you be in a hospital, birthing center, or stay home?

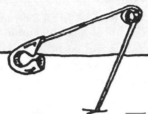

MONTH EIGHT

Pelvic joints expanding, Uterus pressing at the bottom of your rib cage, Your unborn baby starts to head down . . . and out!

TO DO THIS MONTH

- ❑ *Go to childbirth prep classes.*
- ❑ *Take your coach along.*
- ❑ *Schedule a fun day.*
- ❑ *Start seeing your doctor or midwife more often.*
- ❑ *Rethink your exercise routine.*

- ❑ *Add relaxation moves!*
- ❑ *Eat out. . . . Try new restaurants you may want to use for take-out later.*
- ❑ *Rearrange your clothes and raid your mate's closet for items to borrow.*

Your pelvic joints are expanding, your uterus is pressing at the bottom of your rib cage, and your unborn baby starts to head down . . . and out! The big day is getting nearer. As you near the last month of your pregnancy, it is not unusual to experience a bit of anxiety. Fortunately, there are some things you can do as the big event approaches to keep your concerns under control. Organizing things for the hospital—a bag for yourself and one for your baby—is something practical that you can do. At the same time, you can spend time with your childbirth coach. A childbirth coach is a supportive birthing partner. Your coach can be your mate or someone else who knows you well and will be with you to help you through the childbirth process. No matter how intellectually prepared you are for the rigors of giving birth, there's no substitute for a birthing coach.

This Month's Priorities

❏ Go to childbirth prep classes, and take your coach along.
❏ Rethink your exercise routine. Add relaxation moves!
❏ Eat out. . . . Try new restaurants you may want to use for takeout later.
❏ Choose a pediatrician.
❏ Prepare your hospital bag.
❏ Prepare your baby's hospital bag.

Choosing a Name for Your Baby

Many couples find choosing a name for their baby a fun, yet challenging process. It is fun to look up the meanings of all of those possible names for a baby. It may be less fun to legislate the politics of the name—if you name your baby after one grandparent, will the others feel insulted?

Try not to approach the process with your mind set about any particular name or pet peeve about something your mate has in mind. Consider the names on your family trees. Jot down both of your favorites. Browse through some of the great books available (as well as the names in the appendix at the back of this book). Along with all the great books of baby names on store shelves, you will find a veritable wealth of advice and ideas by searching the Internet.

- There are several points to keep in mind when choosing a name for your baby.
- What will your baby's initials spell? You may want to avoid unfortunate acronyms.
- What nicknames go along with the formal name? A name such as Margaret is a good choice for indecisive parents because of the amazing number of possible nicknames.
- What does the name mean? Does it have a positive meaning or historical and cultural associations? Mary, for example, means bitter—hardly a positive designation—but any negativity attached to it for its meaning is outweighed, no doubt, in some parents' minds by its association with Mary, mother of God.
- Do you think it's important to give your baby a common name, or something more unusual? Some people enjoy unusual names, but others, such as my sister Regina, who hated growing up with an uncommon name, deliberately chose to name her daughter Elizabeth, because it was popular.
- Choosing a name for your baby also can be a way of celebrating a common heritage. If you and your mate have one in common.

Above all, keep in mind that your baby's name is something everyone—you, your mate, your baby, and the rest of the family—will have to live with for a long time.

Pediatrician Interview Worksheet

1. What do you find most fulfilling about working with youngsters?

   _____

   _____

2. What kind of regular office policies do you practice? (For instance, are all sick kids sequestered in the same waiting room? Contagious illnesses can spread quickly if this is the case.)

   _____

   _____

   _____

3. What is your philosophy regarding parents? Are you a parent yourself?

   _____

   _____

4. Do you have any rules or regulations regarding emergencies?

   _____

   _____

5. What is the average waiting time for your regular office visits?

   _____

6. Are there any special hours during which you take informational telephone calls from parents?

   _____

7. Will insurance cover all, if not most, of your fees and special requests?

   _____

   _____

Choose a Pediatrician

Don't wait till after your baby is born to choose a pediatrician. A pediatrician can be part of your team when you deliver the baby, checking on your newborn and answering any questions you may have as a brand-new mom. Ask your practitioner to recommend baby doctors. In fact, find out if the doctors on your list have visiting privileges at the hospital or birthing center where you are scheduled for birth.

Friends, family members, and your regular family doctor can also be good sources of great baby doctors. You will also want to check your insurance plan or health maintenance organization for a listing of pediatric practices included in your regular coverage.

To check out a pediatrician, phone first and jot down general impressions. Is the receptionist rude? Do you sense frustration or ridicule in the doctor's voice? You want a professional who will take you as well as your baby's needs seriously. Ask yourself if he or she is a person who respects women, especially new mothers in crises? You don't want to anticipate the worst for your first months of parenting, but you do want to know that your child's doctor will not dismiss your fears or concerns as unfounded. When you get a positive feeling from the staff, set up an appointment to interview the pediatrician. This person will be caring for your child from birth up to age 16. You are interviewing someone for a very important job and not just any name on your list will do.

Hospital Bag Checklist

❑ A robe and nightgown. If you're going to breastfeed, you'll need one that opens easily in the front.

❑ Nonskid slippers. You'll want to make sure that they are nonskid, since hospital floors can be slippery—and you'll be walking to the nursery at least once during your stay.

❑ A nursing bra. Throw in some nursing pads, too, in case your milk comes in sooner than you expect. If you're not

going to breastfeed, bring a bra that's slightly smaller than you would normally wear; this will help your breasts return to their prepregnant state sooner.

❏ Toiletries. Include your toothbrush, toothpaste, hair brush, makeup, and deodorant. Also pack a box of large maxi pads with wings, as you'll need them after the birth.

❏ Comfortable clothing. You'll need one outfit to come home in after the delivery; make sure it's loose enough to accommodate your body comfortably, as you will not loose incredible amounts of weight immediately upon delivery. Include a few pairs of maternity panties and several pairs of socks—you'll need them for the delivery and afterward.

❏ A picture or calming image to focus on. When you're in labor, it helps to have something special to focus on, other than a hospital wall. Bring a favorite nature photo, or maybe one of your pet.

❏ Books, tapes, or magazines. After the birth, you might have a little time to yourself for relaxation. Bring anything you like to help you accomplish that.

❏ A tennis ball or back massager. Especially in labor, you may need your partner to give you a strong back rub. These items will help him provide extra pressure—a godsend if you have back labor.

❏ A bottle of Champagne, or whatever you like to drink, to celebrate baby's arrival.

❏ Your call list. Having all of the names and phone numbers of your friends and family handy will speed the announce-ments along. You'd be surprised how many new parents become so overwhelmed by the birth experience that they forget the numbers of their families and friends; so don't rely on your memory. (Or bring this book!)

❏ Nonperishable snacks for your birthing coach. Your baby's father is bound to get hungry, especially during a long labor, and you don't want him having to spend time waiting on line at the hospital cafeteria when he could be rubbing your back instead. Hospital staff will probably not let you eat during your labor, but there is no reason your partner should starve as well.

❏ A portable CD or tape player and your favorite soothing music. Music during labor can be a big help for relaxation. Your hospital may allow you to play one of these at a low volume, or you could bring along some headphones.

❏ A nursing pillow. If you are planning to nurse, these can be a huge help, and your hospital is unlikely to have them on hand.

❏ A lanolin-based nipple protectant. If you are planning to nurse, this soothing ointment can be a lifesaver, and your hospital may not provide it.

Baby's Hospital Bag Checklist

❏ Two nightshirts. Pack the gowns that are open at the bottom or that have a pull string.

❏ Diapers. If you are planning to shy away from disposables, bring four or five, and be sure to include a waterproof diaper cover to catch any diaper leakage. The hospital will provide all the disposable diapers you will need.

❏ A going-home outfit. By now, you should have lots to choose from. Decide what you want to dress baby in for first pictures, since Dad will probably take several shots of you leaving the hospital. (You might bring along a throwaway camera, too, just in case you forget your "real" one.)

❏ A blanket. Bring a light or heavy one, depending on the climate or the time of year.

❏ A snowsuit. Bring this item only if it's wintertime, of course.

❏ If you're not planning to breastfeed, bring a pacifier. The hospital may give you one, but in case they don't, bring one that's sterilized.

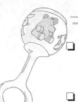

❑ Nail scissors. Most hospitals won't cut baby's nails, which grow quite long in utero. Special baby scissors with clean, sharp edges are the best buy.

❑ A baby hat. The hospital may give you one, but your newborn's head needs to be covered when you walk out the door, no matter what season it is.

How Your Baby Grows

Near the end of this month, your unborn baby could be as long as sixteen and one-half to eighteen inches long and could weigh five pounds. Proportionally, the little body now looks like the head belongs. Fetal heads are disproportionally large for the size of those developing bodies up until the eighth month.

Stockpiling all the immunities, your baby spends some time and energy this month borrowing all that he or she can from you. The natural immunities it has taken you years to build up will help your baby stay healthy during those first few months after birth.

Fatter and bigger, your child doesn't have as much kicking, twisting, or turning room inside the uterus. What used to feel like swooping or swimming inside has now turned into real jabbing and pushing. Stay tuned to those maneuvers now. If you detect less than ten a day, let your doctor know right away. However, as the baby finds less space for physical fun, quiet times may last longer.

Brain cells are just expanding wildly this month and will continue this fast-paced course steadily now. Talk to your baby. Play music. Have your husband or any siblings introduce themselves. These familiar voices and sounds can be heard inside.

Chances of survival outside your body now are marvelous. (If you've been worried about premature labor or have been placed in a high-risk category for any reason, you can feel a bit more comfortable about your body as a baby-making vehicle. Relax . . . you've almost made it to the finish line.)

Gradually shifting to the same position in which 95 percent of all babies are born, your fetus starts to head down, pushing into your pubic area upside down. This move to what is known as the *vertex position* is especially predictable for first births. If your doctor happens to mention that your baby's bottom seems to be descending into your pelvis, as opposed to his or her head, she may be concerned about a *breech birth*, in which the buttocks or feet emerge first.

What You Can Expect to Experience

Emotional Changes

With the birthing process not that far off, it's only natural for you to experience one or more of these very common fears of expectant mothers:

- *Will I have a normal baby?* Statistically speaking, yes, of course. Nature takes care of its own, Lonnie insists, and if you are eating enough of the right foods and taking good care of yourself, then your chances are even greater of having a perfectly normal baby. Even if your child is born with some kind of physical handicap, most conditions are treatable.
- *Will I be overwhelmed by the pain of labor?* There is no way to predict the intensity of your labor and delivery. For most women, the natural birth experience is painful, especially if it is their first time. However, most women also say they "forget" the pain once they experience the joy of knowing their newborn was safely delivered. And, no matter how strenuous the birthing process is, there is no doubt that preparation and attitude go a long way towards helping you to manage it. Reading books, taking classes, and learning to relax and focus will help things go much more smoothly.
- Your pain, if you have any, is going to be manageable because you will be in the hands of a professional you know and trust, and you will have a coach or partner

who is well prepared to take care of you when you are most vulnerable. You will also have the wonders of modern medical pain relief available to you at important points in your progress. If you are still concerned, you may want to try hypnosis. Some practitioners are finding it a useful technique for pain management during the birthing process. Make up your own mind that you will be able to manage anything that comes your way . . . one step at a time.

❧ *Can I get my baby out?* Hipbones have little to do with it. Little, teeny women with teeny hipbones deliver great big babies without episiotomies (*a small snip to widen the perineum before it tears during birth*). Don't forget, only a small percentage of all babies need to be delivered by cesarean section.

❧ *Can I handle the responsibility of a new baby?* This is a fear you will have to work out on your own. Yes, of course, you can handle it, but you have to believe in yourself. There are plenty of good books out there that can help you prepare to raise baby. Start reading them.

As you become bigger, the stares, touches, reactions, and comments of outsiders can catch you off guard and make you wonder why people say or do such stupid things.

❧ "When are you due?" may become one of the most unnerving questions, especially if you have several weeks to go, and you really don't care to share obstetrical details with total strangers. By the way, don't tell people exactly when you are due.

Even if you mentioned the special date way back when, don't broadcast it repeatedly. Or try adding several weeks to the actual date when you tell others. Next month, this fictionalized delivery date will buy you peace and quiet as you draw closer to your rendezvous with a birthday. Everyone who wants to be the first to know will give you more time exactly when you need lots of rest during your ninth month. You won't have to answer the phone as much or return all those messages.

- "You look like you're carrying a . . . [boy? girl? twins?]." New York physician Elizabeth Whelan, M.D. says that statistical analysis has proven that there is no way to tell, short of amniocentesis or X-ray, whether you are carrying a boy or girl, so don't fall victim to old wives' tales.

- "Reach out and touch someone" isn't just an advertising jingle at this point if you've found yourself fending off the touches of people wanting to pat your stomach. Remember, you have a right to your own space, so go ahead and follow your instinct as far as any unwanted gestures are concerned. Put yourself back in your prepregnant state. Would you want this particular person rubbing your stomach for good luck?

- You could also be made to feel as if you've come down with some dreadfully contagious disease because many people shy away from apparently pregnant women. Don't feel ashamed of your marvelous state of being.

- Jokes about your expectant state aren't always funny, so don't feel compelled to laugh or even behave courteously if you don't feel like it. "Soooo Big" is a game you may enjoy later with your baby or toddler, but when adults ogle you now and say, "Oh my, you are soooo big," you don't have to play along.

- Advice givers come out of the woodwork. Use what you like. Throw the rest away quickly, especially if it's negative.

Baby Name Worksheet

BOYS' NAMES		GIRLS' NAMES	
First	Middle	First	Middle

Sample

We welcome with love

_____
(name)

_____
(weight)

_____
(height)

_____
(date)

_____
(your name here)

Write Your Own

_____

_____

_____

_____

_____

_____

Physical Changes

You're Normal If . . .

♂ Your pelvic joints hurt. The pelvis has to stretch for your baby to have room to be born; and in this last trimester, your joints, ligaments, and bones may actually feel sore. The joints loosen up in a rather extraordinary way because of both the hormonal and the physical changes taking place. This remarkable ability is one of the reasons why some very small women are able to give birth to rather large babies. Early in pregnancy, the size of your pelvic joints isn't really a good indication of whether you will be able to deliver vaginally.

♂ Clumsy could be your middle name now, especially when you walk or try to run. You feel downright bulky, but don't always realize how out of balance you really are. In your mind, you may still have that prepregnant body. Don't be hard on yourself emotionally if you start to turn into one of those pregnant ladies who waddles slightly when she walks.

♂ Your underpants could end up wet when you laugh or sneeze. Not only can all this increased pressure on your bladder send you to the bathroom a zillion times each day and into the night, but also sudden quick movements like a laugh or sneeze can make it hard for you to control your urine. This is called *stress incontinence* and is due to the progesterone in your body causing relaxation of the bladder and the sphincter. If you suspect that you are leaking more than urine and the drips could be amniotic fluid, call your doctor and explain your worry right away.

♂ Hemorrhoids could become a real pain. The pressure of your baby's head in your pelvic cavity can cause swollen veins around your anus. If you've been having bouts of constipation during your pregnancy, this hemorrhoidal condition can become a constant, itchy, painful, irksome problem. Hemorrhoids can even bleed. Don't be shy about asking your doctor to recommend help. Put an ice pack against the hemorrhoids. Don't stand in any situation where a seat is possible.

❦ Your breathlessness may have gotten worse. Your uterus might be pressing on the bottom of your rib cage right up on your diaphragm, making you uncomfortable and breathless. Let's face it, your lungs are crowded. Your need to breathe slowly and deeply isn't affecting your baby's growth, unless you are trying to run a marathon. If you are carrying low, breathlessness isn't such a discomfort. Try not to slouch. When you stand or sit up straight, you get more air into your lungs. Prop a pillow up behind you in bed if getting to sleep is a problem.

❦ The veins in your breasts are more prominent.

❦ You've put on lots of your pregnant pounds by now. Although the obstetrical rule of thumb is for your weight gain to start slowing down now, that doesn't always happen. Your womb is still expanding, your placenta is still working its marvelous wonders, your blood volume is up, your baby is putting on pounds, and your overall body fat composition has changed for good reasons. Fat may be concentrated on your hips, breasts, and thighs, and these stores act like nutritional reserve. After delivery, the extra fat helps you become a better breast-feeder. (Even if you aren't going to breastfeed, the fat does tend to drop off in the postpartum period.) Almost all of your baby's weight gain takes place during the last

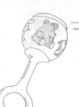

trimester, so please don't limit yourself or try to diet. Are you getting 2,600 calories each day? If not, eat up. If so, pat yourself on the back and don't feel guilty about gaining now.

Taking Care of Yourself

You will be trudging into your practitioner's office more often now, probably every two weeks this month, and then weekly.

Tests for high blood pressure, blood sugar levels, and protein in your urine specimen continue. You'll be watched for any extreme swelling in your hands, feet, or face. Using your own baseline pressure as a gauge, if your blood pressure shoots up more than thirty points in the upper range, or fifteen points in the lower range, this is a sign of preeclampsia, sometimes called *toxemia*, or *pregnancy-induced hypertension*. By now, you've grown accustomed to the cuff, stethoscope, or electronic measurement of your blood pressure.

Checks for a substance called *albumin* in your urine sample, another potential sign of toxemia are also routine by now. Too much albumin indicates trouble. If your level is too high, a special test may be ordered. If your practitioner schedules you for what is called a *glucose tolerance test (GTT)*, blood samples are taken before and after you are given a special glucose drink. The test measures your body's ability to handle sugar in the bloodstream, and can indicate women who may be more likely to have diabetic conditions during their pregnancies. Statistics vary on the number of pregnant women who do end up with gestational diabetes, but this test is often given sometime between the twenty-fourth and twenty-eighth week. If you have shown signs of sugar in your urine earlier or were placed in a high-risk category because of obesity or prior complications in pregnancy, you may already be familiar with the GTT routine. Most blood sugar problems disappear after pregnancy, and because practitioners are now so skilled at recognizing and preparing

for diabetes during pregnancy, most pregnancies proceed without problems. Relax.

Meanwhile, a little extra sugar in your urine isn't out of the ordinary during pregnancy; but if your levels are persistently high, the doctor may be worried about complications from gestational diabetes.

The Nonstress or Antistress Test

To measure fetal heart rate, your doctor can use at least two tests before labor begins: the nonstress test and the contraction stress test, according to the American College of Obstetricians and Gynecologists (ACOG). Both rely on the fetal heart monitor.

A *nonstress test* would measure the heart rate in response to the baby's own movement. Ordinarily, the heart beat speeds up during any kind of activity, even a whoosh or a push by the baby. Any change is considered a good indication of things proceeding along without complications. You lie on a bed or up on an examining table during the procedure for about twenty minutes and press a button every time you feel the baby move. The beats are recorded on a paper and tend to be very reassuring for everyone, especially a worried expectant mom.

A *contraction stress test (CST)* is indicated if the practitioner is concerned about how the baby will react during labor. When your uterus contracts, blood flow to the placenta and to the baby slows down temporarily, so there may be some concern about how effective the placenta is working. If the fetal heartbeat falls with contractions, this is an indication to consider immediate delivery. Blood flow to the placenta decreases with contractions. If the baby cannot maintain a good heart rate during this time, then he or she may be in some degree of distress. During a contraction, the baby's heart, lungs, and systems should be able to survive without any changes for that 40-second length. To initiate mild contractions, you may be given *oxytocin*, a drug to induce laborlike contractions. This procedure can take up to two hours, according to ACOG. Ordinarily, a doctor won't order this unless the nonstress test produces unsatisfactory results. Don't worry about premature labor being induced during the test. Risk is minimal because minimal amounts of oxytocin are used.

If a *biophysical profile* is performed, this just means that the technician used the data to get a clearer picture not only of the fetal heart rate, but also of the baby's muscle tone, body movement, and the amniotic fluid in the womb. Lots of good information can be picked up during a biophysical profile. For instance, although the baby isn't really breathing yet, what experts look for are signs of the little chest moving in and out. Each item in a biophysical profile is scored, and if the number obtained is between eight and ten, then everything is within normal range. Too low a number is cause for concern, and the test may be redone to get a better picture of what's happening. A score of two or less is considered an obstetrical emergency calling for immediate intervention.

A Breech Birth?

If your practitioner brings up the question of a *breech*, or buttocks-first, birth during one of your routine office visits during the last trimester, it's because she or he has felt the hard head of your unborn baby up near your ribs. You may have detected feet or a little bottom down below closer to your pelvis. This unwieldy positioning can definitely shift and change in the next few weeks, and your practitioner may even try to turn the baby using a technique known as *external cephalic version.*

Your practitioner may be concerned because a baby in this breech position is more difficult to deliver and cesarean sections are more likely to ease your baby safely out. Only 3 to 4 percent of babies are born buttocks first. This incidence goes up for premature births. Other factors, such as excessive amniotic fluid, an abnormal

Frank breech

uterus, the location of the placenta, and a history of multiple births, add to the chances of breech positioning.

There are actually three classifications of breech: frank, incomplete, and complete. In *frank breech*, your baby shows up bottom first with his or her legs tucked up close to the chest. The lowest number of breech complications are associated with frank. Theoretically, with an *incomplete breech*, as your cervix dilates in labor, and the baby begins the trip down the birth canal, one or both legs will drop down and will arrive before the rest of the body. You may hear someone describe this as a *single* or *double footling breech birth*. If your baby insists on arriving in what is called a *complete breech*, his bottom is first, but legs and arms are crossed in front of his little body. Another unusual position your practitioner may notice during routine physical exams of your abdomen, also known as palpations, is the *transverse position*, in which the baby is sideways in your womb.

Incomplete breech

Complete (full) breech

RECORD SHEET:
To Our Baby—A Message from Month Eight

PHOTO CAPTION: This picture was taken on_____. It shows

_____.

Dear Baby:
We're getting a little nervous. What will you be like? Who will
you resemble? Here is what we've been thinking about:

_____
_____
_____
_____
_____
_____
_____
_____
_____

Important Reminders	Scheduled Activities "To Do"

Now is the time to . . .

- **Schedule/confirm your monthly checkups with your ob/gyn.** You will be trudging into your practitioner's office more often now, probably every two weeks this month and then weekly. Record your next regularly scheduled checkups on the appropriate dates in this planner!
- **Go to the appointment prepared.** Continue to track your symptoms. Draft a list of any questions you have. Bring both lists to your next doctor's appointment. Expect:
- Tests for high blood pressure, blood sugar levels, and protein in your urine specimen continue.
- To be watched for any extreme swelling in your hands, feet, or face.
- To watch out for a sudden rise in blood pressure. It could be a sign of preeclampsia.

DAY 1

DAY 2

DAY 3

Scheduled Activities "To Do"	Important Reminders

DAY 4

....
....
....
....
....
....
....
....
....
....

DAY 5

....
....
....
....
....
....
....
....
....
....

DAY 6

....
....
....
....
....
....
....
....
....
....

Now is the time to . . .

Practice a "run" to the hospital.
If you live a distance from the hospital, and are worried about getting there on time, there's no time like now to start practicing the trip, even though your chances of not making it to the hospital for delivery on time are low. Most first births don't happen instantaneously. Yet, go ahead and practice at a time when you can map out the best streets and roads to take. Later on, when you are in labor, timing contractions, and trying to stay calm, you'll be glad you know the least stressful route. Figure out which hospital or clinic door you are supposed to enter and ask about filling out any preliminary paperwork beforehand. If you are scheduled to give birth in a big city hospital, be aware of what rush hour traffic congestion will add to your trip's length. Plan ahead. Fill the gas tank of your car and keep it filled. Or, set aside cash for taxis or a car service. Don't forget money for toll roads or bridges if you are going by private car.

Important Reminders	Scheduled Activities "To Do"

Now is the time to . . .

Stop worrying about arriving in time for the birth.

The average first labor lasts from twelve to fourteen hours. Although your 40-minute drive seems to be adding anxiety to your anticipation now, the trip may actually keep your mind occupied, especially if you have done your advance homework and know exactly where you are going and what to expect when you arrive.

DAY 7

DAY 8

DAY 9

Scheduled Activities "To Do"	Important Reminders

DAY 10

....
....
....
....
....
....
....
....
....
....

DAY 11

....
....
....
....
....
....
....
....
....
....
....

DAY 12

....
....
....
....
....
....
....
....
....
....
....

Did You Know . . .

- The size of your pelvic joints isn't really a good indication of whether or not your baby will make an easy appearance?
- Ninety-five percent of all babies are born head-down, or in vertex position?
- You've probably gained about 35 percent of your pregnant weight by now?
- Lamaze birthing ideas are based on a Russian researcher's discovery?
- Ignorance about labor and delivery can actually make it hurt more?
- Lots of expectant couples who can't decide on baby names are using the Internet to gather ideas?

Important Reminders	Scheduled Activities "To Do"

Now is the time to . . .

Look at time as your life

When you stop trying to spend, save, or invest your time, you'll feel less burdened by stress. Of course, your time is important, especially now with only a few weeks to go before your due date, but by looking at it from a rushed, mercenary viewpoint, you may be missing out on so much that is truly enjoyable. You'll never be at this point in your baby-making career again. Find a way to enjoy your time.

DAY 13

DAY 14

DAY 15

Scheduled Activities "To Do"	Important Reminders

DAY 16

....
....
....
....
....
....
....
....
....
....

DAY 17

....
....
....
....
....
....
....
....
....
....

DAY 18

....
....
....
....
....
....
....
....
....
....

Did you know . . .

"An epidural can be used early in labor to help a woman gain control of her fears and the pain. Of course, the best time to insert the epidural is when she has reached four centimeters, but if I have a patient who is extremely worried and can't calm her fears, I'll use it sooner. By using pitocin and a fetal monitor in conjunction with this early epidural, I can even talk the patient through the pushing stage of delivery and she doesn't have to feel anything."
—Howard Berk, M.D.

Important Reminders	Scheduled Activities "To Do"

Important Reminders

Now is the time to . . .

**Buy books and start
reading them to your baby.**

You can begin reading to your baby anytime from conception on. Invest in a small library of books; often you can find great books at bargain prices at your local library book sales. At first, choose books with simple pictures and as few words as possible. Gradually work up to books with simple story lines and rhymes or poetic language. Babies respond well to sounds that are alike, and, for that reason, rhyming stories tend to be most popular with the younger ones.

DAY 19

DAY 20

DAY 21

Scheduled Activities "To Do"	Important Reminders

DAY 22

....
....
....
....
....
....
....
....
....
....
....

DAY 23

....
....
....
....
....
....
....
....
....
....
....
....

DAY 24

....
....
....
....
....
....
....
....
....
....
....
....

Now is the time to . . .

**Have some fun
choosing your baby's name:**
Try:

- Leafing through all the entries in baby name books (such as *The Everything® Baby Names Book*). Try to figure out the names your friends and family would pick if they were allowed to name the baby.
- Hold a lottery. Tell all your friends and relatives that you're looking for suggestions and that you'd like their input. The winner gets to serve as your baby's first sitter when you and your spouse find the time and energy to go out for your first dinner alone after your baby arrives.
- Pick five names that just sound good when you say them. Write them down on a card; and every day for a month, pull the card out and read the names aloud to hear how they sound. At the end of the month, one will probably become your favorite.
- Go through the phone book or the newspaper (the wedding announcements page can be a help) to see if any first names jump out at you.
- Practice yelling different names out the back door, loudly and several times in a row, just before dinnertime. Then ask your neighbors which ones they like best.

Important Reminders	Scheduled Activities "To Do"

Now is the time to . . .

**Try out living
without a second income.**

There are plenty of questions to ask yourself before making a decision as to whether or not to return to the workforce. Weigh all factors before making a final decision. Your reasons for wanting to return to work may be for professional development purposes, but, for many people, it's a financial decision. If you don't feel comfortable analyzing your needs yourself, seek the help of a financial consultant.

Here are some starting points to consider:

- Figure out what you need to live on. Total up all of your monthly living expenses, and don't forget to prorate those items that you pay for once or twice per year (such as taxes and home or car insurance).
- Analyze these expenses against your current and projected new incomes. Can you still meet your monthly obligations if you decide to start a business or stay at home as a full-time parent? Ask yourself whether your income is compatible with your goals.
- Make a new budget, and stick to it. Post it in a conspicuous place (such as on the refrigerator) for everyone in the family to see. This way, everyone knows the financial limitations of the family.

DAY 25

DAY 26

DAY 27

Scheduled Activities "To Do"	Important Reminders

DAY 28

....
....
....
....
....
....
....
....
....
....

DAY 29

....
....
....
....
....
....
....
....
....
....
....

DAY 30/31

....
....
....
....
....
....
....
....
....
....
....

Did you know that . . .

You could have as much as thirteen extra pints of fluid during these last weeks? Friends may say you look a little puffy. This mild swelling in your face, around your eyes, lips, and in your hands and lower limbs is quite common and might be in your lower legs, ankles, and feet. Known as *edema*, it's normal; there's no need to cut down your salt intake. Rest. Nap every day. Watch for signs of extreme and sudden swelling, of course.

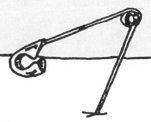

MONTH NINE

Sluggish, uncomfortable, excited, scared . . . You can't imagine how that stomach skin can stretch any further. Worse thought yet: How is this baby going to get out?

TO DO THIS MONTH

☐ *Go out to dinner and to see all the movies you can.*

☐ *Revel in your private time.*

☐ *Buy a new nightgown, robe, and slippers.*

☐ *Discuss pain relief options with your doctor and your mate.*

Your tummy is round and resilient, stretched tight like a drum. Perhaps you've never felt quite so awkward physically. You may find yourself still trying to squeeze into spaces better suited to your former, svelte self. Your lower abdomen is feeling super heavy now, as baby drops down into your pelvis. By now, you're probably feeling a mixture of excitement, fear, and discomfort. How is this baby getting out, you wonder? How much longer will this take? You're tired of going to the bathroom dozens of times a day and through the night . . . not being able to bend down to tie a shoe . . . answering everybody's question, "When are you due?" Additionally, you may struggle with your fears of going through childbirth. Well, instead of focusing on these negatives, do something positive. Give yourself credit for how far you've come. You are in the last stage of one of the most important marathons ever run. You can make it to the finish line! Spend some time every day saying positive affirmations to yourself: "Giving birth comes naturally to me." "I am more than capable of pushing this baby out." And reward yourself. Treat yourself to an outing, a fine meal, or a day of doing nothing at all. You deserve it!

This Month's Priorities

❑ Read up on delivery
❑ Get organized for the first days of new motherhood
❑ Learn the basics of infant care

Pack for Labor Checklist

If you haven't already done so, pack for your hospital stay (see the list in month eight). Keep an open suitcase ready in your bedroom. Be sure to include:

❑ A loose-fitting T-shirt or night gown.
❑ Socks to keep your feet warm.

- ❏ Deodorant and talcum powder.
- ❏ A cosmetic bag packed with toothpaste, a toothbrush, and lip balm.
- ❏ Miscellaneous labor aids, such as a hot water bottle for backaches, a tennis ball for your coach to use to massage you, and a small natural sponge to dip in water for sucking; and your favorite pillow.
- ❏ Books and magazines to read.
- ❏ A clock or watch so you can time contractions.
- ❏ A camera and, if the hospital allows, a video camera to film the big event.

Pack for After the Birth Checklist

You will need:

- ❏ Two to three comfortable cotton night gowns with front openings
- ❏ A comfortable bathrobe
- ❏ Comfortable slippers
- ❏ Brush, comb, shampoo, hairdryer
- ❏ Two boxes of sanitary napkins. You may be dealing with a lot of bloody discharge, called lochia, for several weeks after birth, so stock up now.
- ❏ Breast pads to slip inside your bra for leaky nipples
- ❏ Two to three nursing bras if you plan to breast feed
- ❏ Ointment for sore breasts
- ❏ A comfortable "going home" outfit
- ❏ An infant car seat

Read up on Labor and Delivery

There's a lot to read up on about labor and delivery, but here are some of the highlights. (Read more in the *Everything Pregnancy Book*.)

- Your baby drops down into your pelvis weeks, days, or hours before your body shifts into labor.
- A blob of bloody mucus is eliminated from your cervix, as the cervix starts to open several days before labor, or during the early stages of labor.
- You get diarrhea.
- Your water breaks.
- Contractions arrive in a regular, predictable pattern.
- The cervix flattens and thins out.
- The cervix gradually dilates up to 10 centimeters.
- The amniotic sac breaks.
- Blood from your vaginal face flushes; you feel thirsty.
- You feel an intense backache.
- You feel tired.
- The muscles in your legs could cramp up.
- You feel nauseous and experience chills and shakes.
- Try to synchronize your pushing efforts. Medical staff will tell you when to push for maximum effect.
- The baby's head crowns.
- Your vagina stings as it is stretched to the max.
- You feel a gush, and the rest of the baby's body slides out.
- The baby cries.
- The baby is placed on your stomach.
- The umbilical cord is clamped and then cut.
- Your uterus continues to contract until the placenta is expelled.

Get Organized for New Motherhood

- Stockpile basic food items.
- Plan easy to cook or reheatable frozen meals
- Post menus from take out restaurants and restaurants that deliver.
- Arrange for a cleaning service.
- Arrange for help in the form of a nurse, nanny, or relative.

Infant Care Basics

Feeding Baby

Your baby's first-ever need from you is food. Many babies, in fact, feed in those first few moments after birth. But whether you choose to breastfeed or bottlefeed, there are plenty of important considerations to mull over prior to making a decision. You'll need as much information as possible to ensure that the final decision is one that you feel good about and that baby draws the most benefit from in the long run.

You've probably heard from both sides on the issue of breast feeding. Some mothers (and some doctors) will tell you that breastfeeding is the only way to make sure that baby is getting proper nutrition. Others will say that formula feedings now contain better nutrients.

Both of these arguments are actually right. Formula is better than it has ever been, and breastmilk provides excellent protection against illnesses.

So, what's a new parent to do? All things being equal, it really boils down to your own personal comfort level and belief system. If you don't feel comfortable with the way you are feeding your baby, your discomfort level will become evident to the baby, and you could wind up with some feeding problems.

Breastfeeding

Breastfeeding is the most highly recommended form of providing proper nutrition for your baby. Your own milk not only has the right amount of fat and nutrients to help baby grow, but also contains compounds that help build baby's immune system.

Nursing your baby should begin immediately upon birth, to give you and baby a chance to get used to this new method of meeting baby's nutritional needs. Remember that up until this point, baby has only fed on your food and prenatal vitamins—and had room service delivered it via the umbilical cord!

Now, your baby has to work a little bit harder for his or her food. So, when you first begin to breastfeed, expect that it may take a few tries before the two of you get the hang of it. Invest in the services of a lactation consultant who can ease your mind by showing you the proper positions for breastfeeding and how to tell if baby has a good latch.

Contrary to popular belief, breastfeeding is not as easy as it looks—at first. What we are made to believe comes naturally may often be trial and error until we get used to it; so don't lose your cool until you're absolutely sure there's a problem that will permanently impede your breastfeeding efforts.

Mastitis (a painful infection of the milk ducts) is one reason mothers stop nursing their babies; the only other common reason for discontinuing nursing is the mother's belief that she'll never get it right. In the latter case, try not to give up until you've discussed the problem with your doctor or a lactation consultant, since it may be an easy problem to fix.

Here are some breastfeeding tips:

- Start in a quiet, peaceful environment. Make sure to get visitors to leave while you're nursing your baby, at least until you feel more confident. There's nothing worse than being a proud new mom and then having nursing difficulty while feeling pressure to "perform." Peaceful concentration on baby will help the milk flow easily.
- Nurse as often as you can, primarily every time the baby seems hungry. At the hospital, if you are sure you want to nurse exclusively, be sure to point this out clearly to the neonatal nurses. So often, well-meaning nurses offer to feed

the baby glucose water or formula so that you can rest. If you don't want this to happen, be clear and direct in your instructions that baby be brought to you every time he or she seems hungry. The more you nurse, the more milk you will produce. Experts agree that you should try to feed at least eight times per day.

The first few days, you will not see (or feel) a whole lot of milk. However, your pre-milk has plenty of immunities in it for your baby to consume, and baby actually doesn't need much more in the first days. It takes regular stimulation to make more milk. When your milk is delivered, you'll know it: Your breasts will swell, and they may even feel like cool water is running through them. Some women report a tingling feeling. Whatever symptom you experience, you'll know it's time for feeding your baby when your breasts are ready.

Pretend that your breast is a target; the nipple is the bullseye, but the areola surrounding it is the rest of the target. Position your baby's chin and nose against your breast, and then make sure baby gets the whole target in his or her mouth. If you just let baby attach to your nipple, you will not have a good latch; and while your baby can still get milk, your nipples will feel like they are nearly being pulled off of your body. If you see tiny sores on your nipples, you likely aren't positioning baby correctly, and your nipples are probably starting to abscess.

Nurse for about 10 minutes on each side to encourage milk production in both breasts. Also, drink lots of fluid before, during, and after feeding. You need to stay hydrated in order to produce more milk and to keep your own body in a healthy balance.

- Once you're home, keep your baby in a bassinet next to your bed. That way, you don't have far to go when he or she gets hungry in the middle of the night. And breastfeeding babies nearly always will be hungry a few times at night.
- If you experience breast pain, alternate hot and cold packs on your breasts. I know some women who used frozen vegetable packages, because they are cold yet extremely flexible. Use whatever works.
- To build up nipple durability and keep from getting too tender, try squeezing a little bit of breastmilk and rubbing it into your nipples. Let the milk air dry. This offers your nipples natural protection from dry or chapped skin. Another solution is to use lanolin cream on your breasts; it provides a safe, harmless barrier to skin problems.
- Cradle your baby's head, but not so closely that baby can't turn away from you when he or she is finished eating. It's baby's only way of telling you he or she is done.
- Be sure to follow your prenatal diet (and stay on the vitamins as long as you're breastfeeding). Eat a well-balanced diet, and keep the fluids coming. Don't drink too much fluid, however, since this can defeat the purpose. A dozen or more servings a day is probably too much.

If you have problems that seem persistent or if you'd just like some friendly support, call the La Leche League at 1-800-LALECHE (or visit their Web site at *http://www.prairienet.org/llli*).

The benefits of breastfeeding are not limited to baby. You can also reap some rewards, including weight loss (if you breastfeed for at least three months); a uterus that contracts more quickly (since feeding stimulates contraction); and a lower chance of breast cancer (for you and, believe it or not, for female babies who were breastfed). Also, breastfed babies tend to spit up less than formula-fed babies do.

Best of all, it's free and always available, no matter where you are. You can also use a breast pump for times you can't be there, to ensure that baby is getting breastmilk at all times.

The Positives of Formula Feeding

What if you decide, for a health reason or just plain convenience, that baby will be formula fed? Should you feel like you have to explain it to everyone who asks? The decision to feed your baby formula is a personal one; and whether or not other folks agree, formula is better than ever at mimicking breastmilk in terms of nutrients.

The first discussion about formula feeding should be with your partner. If you both agree this is the way to go, then you need to talk with your pediatrician about the appropriate formula for your baby. Many pediatricians suggest using cow's milk formula with iron; however, if your baby has an intolerance to cow's milk, you will need to switch to a soy-based formula. Neither is a poor choice; it just depends on what baby's specific needs are.

Here are some tips for hassle-free formula feeding:

- If you can, buy the premixed cans of formula. These are the easiest to use, since they are already of perfect consistency. I've found that the powders take too long, are messy, and often don't mix well (especially after the bottles are refrigerated). The premixed formula costs a little more; but believe me, it's worth it when you have a crying baby at 2 a.m. and no bottles are ready.
- Alternate the positions you feed baby in, for variety and proper balance on your arm muscles.
- Sterilize all bottle pieces thoroughly, and always keep your hands and kitchen area clean. Use antibacterial soap to clean.

- Feed baby every three or four hours the first few months. Follow what your pediatrician tells you about increasing frequency or when to add cereal to the mix.
- Don't heat the formula in the microwave. Instead, put warm water into a dish or bowl, and then place the bottle inside. This will help the formula heat up uniformly—and prevent burns for baby.
- Tip the bottle over and sprinkle some formula onto your wrist to make sure it's the right temperature. Lukewarm is good.
- Don't reuse formula if baby doesn't drink the whole bottle of milk. Using a bottle over again promotes bacterial growth, which is not desirable with a little one.
- From birth to about four months, feed baby 4 to 6 ounces of formula at a feeding. Many doctors are starting babies on solid foods after four months.
- Stop halfway throughout the feeding and burp the baby. Burp again after baby is done eating. Keep the bib on for about fifteen minutes after feeding. Formula-fed babies often spit up in that time frame, and you'll want to be ready.
- Enjoy your bonding time with baby every bit as much as you would if you were breastfeeding. Cuddle, kiss, and love the baby while feeding; and share the joy of bonding with your baby with others in your family. Let all who ask have a try at feeding baby (with the exception of small siblings who aren't ready to hold baby yet).

When your baby reaches the age of four months, your pediatrician may recommend that you start him or her on solid foods. You'll start with something easy, such as rice or oatmeal, before moving on to jars of baby food and finger foods.

Tackling the Diaper Dilemma
One of the first choices you'll make as a new parent is which type of diaper to use on your baby. Here are your options:

- Your own cloth diapers. You can purchase a set of fifty or more diapers and wash them for reuse. Your baby may go through six to eight diapers per day. *Pros:* You can save a lot of money on diapers. *Cons:* It's a lot more work, and you'll go through tons of heavy-duty detergent in the process. Some reports indicate that home washing machines don't sterilize the same way commercial units do. Also, cloth diapers often leak, leading to more wet clothes.
- A diaper service. You can hire a service that drops off clean new diapers and removes the dirty ones once per week. *Pros:* It's convenient and environmentally responsible. *Cons:* It's costly and annoying, particularly if you miss your dirty diaper pickup.
- Disposable diapers. You can buy these virtually anywhere, and their manufacturers claim that they are friendlier than ever to the environment. *Pros:* They are convenient and readily available; these diapers are also great for travel. *Cons:* They can be expensive.

The "bottom" line is this: You should choose what is most comfortable for the baby and convenient for you.

Diapering Tips

- Take off the dirty diaper, wipe away as much stool as you can with the front of the diaper, and use a warm wash cloth or baby wipes for the rest.
- Be aware of the differences between boys and girls, and wipe accordingly. For girls, you should always wipe from front to back (and never in the opposite direction) to prevent any debris from getting into the vagina. Even baby girls can get bladder, urinary tract, or kidney infections, and fecal matter in the vaginal area is a primary cause. For baby boys, clean a circumcised penis with warm water and apply

a thin layer of petroleum jelly to the tip. For boys who have not been circumcised, pull the foreskin back and wash with a warm cloth.

- Let the baby "air dry" without a diaper for a few minutes to minimize the chance of diaper rash. Then apply some petroleum jelly to the diaper area to keep baby's skin soft and protect it from irritation.

Bathing Baby

Bathing a newborn can be a challenge, but it can be one of the most fun times you have with your baby. Of course, when you're reading about it, it will look easy; but you may find it difficult at first if you're not used to a wet little one trying to squirm out of your arms. Try to keep calm, and have your partner with you (at least the first time) for backup assistance.

Your baby should have a complete bath about once or twice per week but should also be sponged off every day. Use a sponge or warm cloth with baby soap to wipe away any dirt, excess formula, or body oil.

Feed your baby at least an hour before the bath, so that he or she can relax and go to sleep after a pleasant bathing experience— and so that you can avoid any unpleasant surprises in the diaper region.

Here are a few more tips:

- Bathe your baby in a warm bathroom. This will help drain baby's sinuses, and it will cut down on the chances of baby catching a chill.
- Keep all bath supplies within immediate reach, including that rubber ducky you've been saving for baby's special moment.
- Put baby's towel on the floor (preferably on top of the soft bathroom rug) so that you have your hands totally on the baby as you take her or him out of the tub. Wet

babies can slip easily, and especially so if you have to let one hand go to reach for the towel.

Here are some tips on how to give baby a sponge bath:

- Fill a bowl or small bucket with lukewarm water. Put a sponge in the water, and add a little baby bath if you want to.
- Place a large bath towel on a flat surface (such as a bed, carpeted floor, or kitchen counter). Put the baby on the towel, folding a part of the towel over the baby to keep the warmth in. Be sure to keep one hand over the baby at all times.
- Wash the baby's face and the rest of his or her body. Be gentle, talk to the baby to comfort him or her, and don't move too quickly. Wipe the baby gently to dry.
- Dress the baby, and then soothe him or her by rocking and singing a lullaby. You've both earned a nice rest.

Putting Baby to Sleep

You've heard the horror stories. Like the one where you put the baby to bed, and all seems well. But then you hear an unmistakable cough, then sputter—then "WAAAAAA!" You wonder what could possibly have happened in those first few minutes to make your baby change from a contented little angel to a holy terror. Or you just begin to relax and wind down for the evening, finally getting the chance to read the previous morning's paper (it's not uncommon!), when suddenly you hear the baby crying louder and louder, until you just can't stand it anymore. What can you do to get this baby back to sleep?

There are plenty of reasons why some babies don't sleep through the night. The baby could have gas, or have teeth coming, or just want to be rocked in your arms for comfort. Some babies don't sleep well at night because they are allowed to sleep for long stretches during the day. And some babies are just plain colicky.

Ten Ways to Calm a Crying Newborn

1. Determine whether the baby is hungry. Sixty percent of the time, an empty tummy is what makes a baby cry. Offer a bottle or a breast.

2. Check baby's diaper. Change the diaper as quickly and quietly as you can; making a big fuss over the diaper can actually irritate baby more.

4. Swaddle or wrap the baby tightly in a blanket, just as the nurses did in the hospital nursery. Place the blanket sideways, with a point at the top. Next, place the baby at the top point, and then tuck one side under the baby's body. Pull up the bottom fold, and then wrap the remaining side over the baby's body. You're not cutting off circulation here, but you are providing that feeling of womb-like security for your baby.

5. Give the baby a pacifier. Like them or not, they are often temporary solutions to crying problems.

6. Try to work out tummy gas. Put the baby on his or her stomach, and gently rub baby's back or pat baby's bottom. Or lay baby on his back while gently moving his legs back and forth. Use gas drops (available over the counter) as a last resort.

7. Give the baby a warm bath. There's nothing so soothing as a warm tub. Many babies calm down as soon as they hit the water. Add an infant massage, and you'll have yourself one calm baby.

8. Give the baby a song and dance. Try singing to your baby, and move around the room as you do so. Babies have short attention spans, and can be easily redirected.

9. Take baby for a walk or a ride in the car. Babies love motion, and the motion of an automobile somehow serves as anesthesia for babies. You'd be surprised to know how many miles are put on a car just for a baby's sake.

10. Put baby to bed. Like all of us, baby can get irritable when tired. Since their bodies are so much smaller than ours, they process food and milk differently and thus get sleepy

more quickly than you might think. Put on the baby's lullaby tape or music box, dim the lights, and then walk out. Older babies over six months can be left to cry for at least ten minutes before you return to the room (unless, of course, you're absolutely convinced there's really something wrong). Some crying before falling asleep is normal for most babies.

The Baby Sleep Cycle and How It Is Different from Ours

Many first-time parents believe (mistakenly) that babies are supposed to sleep all day and night until they are a few months old. This is not true. Babies, especially newborns, do require lots of sleep to grow, but they should only sleep at two- to three-hour intervals during the day. The main reason for waking your baby, if he or she is sleeping longer than three hours at a stretch, is to make sure the baby is getting proper nourishment. If the baby is not getting enough food at regular times throughout the day, it will only serve to make your nights longer.

Keys to Baby Relaxation

There are two basic words to remember when trying to calm your baby into sleeping mode: atmosphere and routine.

- Atmosphere. Dim the lights, put on soft lullaby-by-the-sea tapes, and rock your baby to sleep. Let your baby feel your heartbeat; it's calming and comforting to the baby, reminding him or her of that special time in the womb.
- Routine. Stick to your routine with the baby as much as possible. Write it down if you find it hard to remember. Figure out ways to stick with your routine even when you're on the road—stop and feed your baby at the same time you would

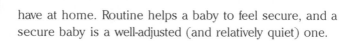

have at home. Routine helps a baby to feel secure, and a secure baby is a well-adjusted (and relatively quiet) one.

Call your pediatrician if your baby just doesn't seem right or isn't responding to any of the suggested methods of calming. Your pediatrician may be able to help you with other suggestions.

How Your Baby Grows

Your baby is gaining as much as one ounce a day now and could weigh as much as five to six pounds. In length, your baby can be more than eighteen inches long. By Week 40, he may weigh more than seven and one-half pounds and be twenty inches in length.

Fat deposits plump out your baby's skin. Nails have grown to the tips of her tiny fingers and toes. If it's a boy, the testicles have descended. (You can see them in ultrasound images.) Arms and legs are in a flexed position. Lungs are fully mature. The lanugo—or downy hair, as well as the cheesy protective coating, or vernix—covering the body, is disappearing. A dark, tarlike substance called merconium is in your baby's intestines and will become the contents of his or her first bowel movement. Hair might have grown as much as two inches, and skin starts to have color.

As you near your due date, your baby won't be quite so active. (However, if your baby is in trouble, he or she will also try to conserve energy by staying too quiet.) Take a half-hour after you awake in the morning and before retiring at night to sit still and count the number of kicks. Even 10 moves a day are fine.

What You Can Expect to Experience

This month is a month where emotions are bound to swing from the highest highs to the lowest lows. The beginning of the month is a continuation of all the months before; the end of the month is the culmination of all your efforts for nearly a year, and perhaps the crowning moment of your life. But up until the drama of the actual birth, consider yourself normal if . . .

- Your lower abdomen feels heavy
- Your cervix is softening and getting ready to dilate, or open to let the baby out. Your vagina has stretched and increased in length. It may take on a purplish hue, due to being engorged with blood. Secretions from you cervix may cause an increase in vaginal discharge.

Taking Care of Yourself

- Good posture will help your balance, which is being thrown off by your baby.
- Don't lie flat on your back. Getting into a prone position can take your breath away or make you feel sick to your stomach.
- Moisturize your breasts and expanding belly.
- Slow down; relax. The hormones in your body when you are stressed can cause early contractions, at least in theory.
- Put your feet up whenever you can to cut down on edema. One report indicated that a dip in a shoulder-deep pool of cool water also can help to relieve edema.

RECORD SHEET:
To Our Baby—A Message from Month Nine

PHOTO CAPTION: This picture was taken on_____. It shows

_____.

Dear Baby:
Here you are! You're the most beautiful baby we've ever seen! We love you!

Important Reminders

Now is the time to . . .

- Schedule/confirm checkups with your ob/gyn. Record your next regularly scheduled checkups on the appropriate dates in this planner!
- Stockpile food and sundries for your first weeks home after giving birth.
- Pack for the hospital
- Confirm hospital policies
- Compile a list of calls to make to announce the birth from the hospital
- Decide on whether to use a diaper service

Scheduled Activities "To Do"

DAY 1

DAY 2

DAY 3

Scheduled Activities "To Do"	Important Reminders
DAY 4	*Did you know that . . .* Taking a bath during the last weeks of pregnancy used to be prohibited because of fear of infection from dirty water? This warning is no longer considered appropriate; your baby is well protected by a plug of mucus and the amniotic sac (unless they are eliminated).
DAY 5	
DAY 6	

Important Reminders	Scheduled Activities "To Do"

Now is the time to . . .

Stop worrying about getting your figure back after the birth.
No matter how much weight you gain, relax. A lot of it will disappear, soon. Keep in mind that 38 percent is the baby, 22 percent is blood and fluid, and 20 percent is pure womb, buttocks, legs, and breasts.

DAY 7

DAY 8

DAY 9

Scheduled Activities "To Do"	Important Reminders

DAY 10

....
....
....
....
....
....
....
....
....
....

DAY 11

....
....
....
....
....
....
....
....
....
....
....

DAY 12

....
....
....
....
....
....
....
....
....
....
....

Now is the time to . . .

Buy a car seat. A baby car seat is required by law. In fact, you won't be able to leave the hospital with your baby unless you have one. You have the option of buying a car seat that is strictly for infants (rear-facing only, handling infants up to twenty pounds) or one that is for both infants and toddlers (can convert to front-facing and holds an infant or toddler up to forty-five pounds). For the sake of convenience, look for one that is portable.

Important Reminders	Scheduled Activities "To Do"

Did you know that . . .

Your amniotic membranes can rupture before labor begins? In fact, the water breaks first for 10 percent of all pregnant women, and most often at night.

DAY 13

DAY 14

DAY 15

Scheduled Activities "To Do"	Important Reminders

DAY 16

....
....
....
....
....
....
....
....
....
....
....

DAY 17

....
....
....
....
....
....
....
....
....
....
....

DAY 18

....
....
....
....
....
....
....
....
....
....
....

Now is the time to . . .

- Read through the signs of labor one more time
- Make sure emergency numbers are posted prominently near telephones
- Schedule nap times. Get plenty of rest.
- Do relaxation exercises.
- Put the finishing touches on your baby's room.
- Pick out something pretty to wear on your first day as a new mother.

Important Reminders

Now is the time to . . .

Sit down with your practitioner and review all your options for pain relief. Get a professional description of each type of pain medication available. Pain relief during labor and delivery falls into two catagories: analgesics or anesthetics. Analgesics (Meperidine, Demerol, Seconal, and Valium) relax you, make you drowsy or high, and make you relax between contractions. They work by depressing your system. Anesthetics eliminate pain either through induction of the semiconscious (general anesthesia) or by interrupting the pathway of nerves that carries the sensation of pain to the brain. In addition to general anesthesia, the options include balanced anesthesia (a combination of drugs, each dosage sufficient to produce its own desired effects) and local or regional anesthesia, which includes the epidural, in which an anesthetic is administered by inserting a needle between two vertebrae of your lower back when you are well into labor.

DAY 19

DAY 20

DAY 21

Scheduled Activities "To Do"	Important Reminders
DAY 22	*Now is the time to . . .* **Ask your doctor what's in store for you when you arrive at the hospital or birthing center.** Steps the nursing staff may routinely take to get you ready for delivery could include shaving your pubic hair, administering an enema to empty your bowls, hooking you up to an intravenous line to administer fluids as well as analgesics and anesthetic agents, or hooking you up to a fetal monitor.
DAY 23	
DAY 24	

Important Reminders

Now is the time to . . .

Watch for signs of labor. They include:

- Contractions arriving every fifteen to twenty minutes and lasting sixty to ninety seconds.
- A cervix dilated to four or five centimeters

Scheduled Activities "To Do"

DAY 25

DAY 26

DAY 27

Scheduled Activities "To Do"	Important Reminders
DAY 28	***Now is the time to . . .***
	• Call the hospital when contractions start arriving every five minutes to alert them that you'll soon be on your way, so you can settle any paperwork before you arrive.
	• Go to the hospital when your contractions start arriving every five minutes or are painful
	• Give birth!
	• Take your baby home.
	• Adjust to life as a new mother.
DAY 29	
DAY 30/31	

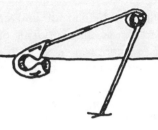

APPENDIX A

Answers to
Commonly Asked Questions

Will the bottle of champagne I shared with my husband on the night we conceived our baby be harmful?

Put this night of celebration behind you and stop feeling guilty. Guilt is a waste of your time now. Binge drinking or regular abuse of alcohol when you are pregnant can cause birth defects, but an isolated episode of too much champagne probably has not harmed your unborn baby.

Ashley Wivel, a medical student at the Yale University School of Medicine, on the Internet site, *Caring/Hygeia*, an Online Journal for Pregnancy and Neonatal Loss (http://hygeia.org), says that one in every three hundred babies is born with some sign of what is known as *fetal alcohol syndrome (FAS)* because their mothers drank on a regular basis during pregnancy. Heavy drinking, including binges or daily use, is especially associated with congenital defects. Babies born with FAS show retarded growth, have central nervous system problems, and certain characteristic facial features, including a small head, a thin upper lip, a short upturned nose, a flattened nasal bridge and a general underdeveloped look of the face. Because of the critical nervous system involvement, many show tremulousness, can't suck, are hyperactive, have abnormal muscle tone, and are later diagnosed with attention deficit disorder as well as mental retardation.

Relying on alcohol out of habit or cravings can also end your pregnancy abruptly. Heavy to moderate drinkers seem to experience a higher incidence of miscarriage in the second trimester, as well as problems with the placenta. Other complications linked to alcohol use are congenital heart defects, brain abnormalities, spinal and limb defects, and urinary and genital problems.

What should you take for a headache?

Aspirin is fine for most of your pregnancy. Avoid it in the last month. Tylenol, or an analgesic based on acetaminophen, is also recommended for headaches.

I have terrible allergies. Is there anything at all my doctor is going to be able to recommend?

For some women, pregnancy can feel like a bad head cold. The increased volume of blood to your mucus membranes can make the lining of your respiratory tract swell. You may even see increased nosebleeds. Fortunately, there are safe medications available to ease the symptoms, so consult with your doctor. See about taking extra vitamin C. A humidifier can be helpful. Packing the nostril with gauze and then pinching your nose between your thumb and forefinger can treat nosebleeds. To shrink the blood vessels and reduce bleeding, try putting an ice pack on your nose.

If I develop an infection, are there any antibiotics safe for expectant moms?

Yes, pharmaceutical companies are coming up with new antibiotics all the time, and a number of them are safe for pregnancy. According to Dr. Lauerson, "Natural and synthetic penicillins are the safest antibiotics to take during pregnancy," so if you are not allergic to these oldest weapons against infection, you are definitely in luck. If you do get sick, make sure that your obstetrician is aware of anything your family doctor or another specialist may be prescribing.

What are my chances of having twins?

If twins run in your family, you certainly have an increased chance of doubling your pregnancy efforts. Yet, if you did not take fertility drugs to get pregnant, your likelihood of naturally conceived twins has actually dropped in recent years. Fertility treatments do increase the chances that you will become pregnant with more than one baby.

You will have fraternal twins if two separate eggs are fertilized by two separate sperm. Three times more common than identical twins, and based on heredity, these fraternal fetuses have their own placentas, may even be different sexes, and may not look more like each other than ordinary brothers and sisters in the same family.

When a single fertilized egg separates into two distinct halves, identical twins are the result. These unborn babies share the same placenta, are always the same sex, and will have the same genetic makeup and similar physical characteristics.

Carrying two or more babies will put a lot more stress on your body, and your doctor is going to monitor you much more closely than if you were expecting one baby. Early detection of the babies using ultrasounds and by taking blood tests to measure your hormone levels will help keep you on track.

What are the dangers of X-rays to my unborn baby?

The dangers of X-rays really rise when someone has a malignancy and needs treatment doses of radiation. If I have a patient who comes into the office early in pregnancy and says, "Oh, Dr. Berk, I've just had a series of X-rays for diagnostic purposes and I didn't know I was pregnant, what should I do?" I advise her to do nothing because there is no need to do anything. Those doses don't cause a lot of problems," says Howard Berk, M.D. However, if you are a dental practitioner, you should definitely bring up your concerns with your doctor. A dentist's office can be an unsafe place for your unborn child. Exposure to radiation, nitrous oxide (laughing gas), and mercury is dangerous. Even sitting in front of a computer all day can be somewhat unhealthy due to low-level radiation.

Is there anything my husband and I may have done that might influence our baby's sex?

Although men don't always want to know this, they hold the key to the baby's sex, not you. Men have two different kinds of sperm, male and female. The most recent research news on choosing the sex of your baby comes from investigators in Fairfax, Virginia, who have been able to presort sperm based on DNA and help couples produce baby girls. Sperm carrying the X chromosome, which creates a female, are actually heavier than those carrying the Y chromosome. Their results, published in the journal *Human Reproduction* and based on a U.S. Department of Agriculture method developed for farm animals, aren't yet perfect but are dramatically close to being accurate in preselecting the sex of a baby. If you are at risk for having a baby with a genetic disease that could be avoided by prechoosing the child's sex, then this new option is good news. A number of genetic disorders affect only males, for instance, and for couples legitimately worried about such outcomes, the Genetics and IVF Institute's fertility research could be most welcome.

I have epilepsy and have been seizure free for several years thanks to my medication. Can I still take my antiepileptic drugs and deliver a healthy baby?

Many obstetricians and pharmacologists get very worried when you mention the words pregnancy and epilepsy in the same context. However, when you speak to an epileptologist (a doctor specializing in seizure treatment), the news is not all doom and gloom. Andrew Wilner, M.D., of The Neurology Foundation, Providence, RI, and author of *Epilepsy, 199 Answers*, explains, "Although medications can cause birth defects, they usually do not. The risk of birth defects in children to women with epilepsy is about 6 percent. That means there is a 94 percent chance there will be no birth defects." Dr. Wilner suggests that you sit down with your specialist and plan your pregnancy very carefully, making certain not to begin or stop taking any medications without serious consideration. "The risk of harm to you and your baby is probably greater if you have a convulsion than the risk to your baby from medication." He also explains that pregnancy is a good time to reevaluate the drugs you may be taking. Your body will be undergoing profound biochemical changes and you may even want to have the drug levels in your blood checked much more frequently than in your recent past. You really want to take "the least number of drugs at the lowest dosages to control your seizures."

Can Ultrasounds Ever Give Misleading Information?

Occasionally, parents wonder about the accuracy of the information obtained from an ultrasound. "Is the baby really a boy?" If the sonogram indicates a due date that seems wrong, you might ask, "Could I possibly have dated the start of my pregnancy incorrectly?" Experts say that if the ultrasound is done at sixteen weeks and beyond, results are pretty accurate, although the equipment and the skill of the technician are factors to be considered. When an ultrasound is scheduled during the first trimester (in the first twelve weeks of your pregnancy), the accuracy drops a bit. A very clear image must be obtained for the ultrasound to determine whether you are expecting a boy or a girl, for instance. This may be more difficult to see in the early stages. Don't worry, most technicians won't say for certain unless they are absolutely certain. When dating the length of a pregnancy, the ultrasound technician can be accurate within a few days. Ultrasounds also date your pregnancy from the point of conception, which is a few days different from the point of your last period.

My dreams seem more vivid now that I'm pregnant. Is there a connection?

Although there are no studies to confirm the connection between elevated hormones and very active dream states, vivid and emotionally powerful dreams are typical during pregnancy and immediately after delivery. In addition to body chemistry affecting your nighttime imagination, the simple fact of facing a life-altering event is having an impact. If you can clearly recall your dream upon awakening, analysts suggest that you try to figure out the emotion behind the dream. Dreaming in pregnancy can be a way for you to face deep emotions. If the feelings connected to your dreams are at all worrisome to you, consult your doctor, a good friend, or counselor.

Why am I so hot and sweaty?

Your metabolism works overtime during pregnancy. Your body is burning more calories. An increase in blood supply to the surface of your skin, as well as hormones, all have an affect on how hot you feel. Keep cool by dressing in natural fibers. Layer clothes. Hop in the shower; pat on a little talcum powder afterwards. You may need to change antiperspirants if your normal brand isn't working. To avoid dehydration, drink plenty of water.

Why am I such a scatterbrain?

Increased hormones can make your thinking a bit foggy—just as they can during your menstrual cycle. You are not going crazy. Stop trying to aim for perfection. Manage the situation by reducing your stress load, making lists, and going easy on yourself.

What is toxoplasmosis, and should I worry about getting it?

Toxoplasmosis is rare, but it is a virus that can affect your baby in the womb. When cats are allowed to run freely outside they can end up with a parasite that settles in the intestines and is secreted into litter boxes. If you catch toxoplasmosis, there is a 40 percent chance your baby will be born blind, deaf, or mentally handicapped. If cats are housebound, there is less reason for concern. To avoid this illness, don't clean any litter boxes. Your doctor also can determine through a blood test whether you have previously had toxoplasmosis and are carrying antibodies.

Can sugar substitutes cause problems during pregnancy?

The Food and Drug Administration and the American Academy of Pediatrics agree that aspartame and saccharin are safe, but unless you have diabetes and need to control your sugar intake, there is no good reason to consume a lot of artificial sweeteners.

My doctor recommends lots of iron, but it makes me feel nauseous. What should I do?

Take iron-rich prenatal vitamin supplements between meals with plenty of water or along with a fruit juice rich in vitamin C, which enhances the absorption of iron. Avoid drinking milk, coffee, or tea with iron. Add liver, red meat, fish, and poultry to your diet to increase dietary iron.

What kings of food cravings are normal?

Many pregnant women crave sweet or salty foods. Cravings for bizarre substances such as baking soda, starch, or coffee grounds are different. A phenomenon called *pica*, which has shown up in medical literature since the sixth century, results in strange cravings that can result in problems for a pregnant mother and her unborn baby. If you have a craving to eat clay, ashes, laundry starch, or other unusual substances, seek medical attention right away.

Can my car's seatbelt harm my unborn baby?

Automobile accidents are a leading cause of death among pregnant women. You should always wear your seatbelt when in a moving vehicle. Seatbelts are designed to accommodate 400-pound men, so you should be able to adjust your belt to suit you. Don't worry about your belt putting pressure on your baby. The baby is well protected by amniotic fluid and layers of tissue, muscle, and fat.

Does intercourse hurt the baby?

Unless you are in a high-risk category, you are not going to harm your baby by making love. Sex is quite safe in a normal pregnancy. Vaginal bleeding, a history of miscarriage or premature labor, or a diagnosis of placental problems are good reasons to restrict lovemaking, however. During the last month before your due date, you also should proceed with caution. Ask your practitioner if you have any concerns.

Should I circumcise my baby?

Whether or not to circumcise your baby is a highly personal decision. Technically, circumcision is removal of the foreskin that covers the head of the penis. The procedure takes only a few minutes to complete but is painful. A majority of boys are circumcised during the first days or weeks after birth, some for religious reasons, others for social reasons. A 1989 study by the American Academy of Pediatrics found that uncircumcised boys were more likely to suffer from urinary tract infections.

How soon can I have sex after the baby's birth?

Many doctors recommend waiting four to six week, but every couple is different. Very few couples are able to swing back into a sex life immediately after the birth of a baby. The important thing is to keep lines of communication open with your mate and to spend intimate time together.

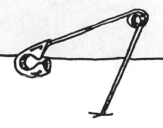

APPENDIX B

Important Addresses

Useful Names and Addresses

Baby's Father

Office address:

Telephone Number:

Dentist

Name:

Address:

Phone Number:

Family Physician

Name:

Address:

Phone Number:

Gynecologist

Name:

Address:

Phone Number:

Hospital

Name:

Address:

Phone Number:

Midwife

Name:

Address:

Phone Number:

Visiting Nurse Service

Name:

Address:

Phone Number:

Obstetrician

Name:

Address:

Phone Number:

Pediatrician

Name:

Address:

Phone Number:

Other Medical Staff

Title:

Name:

Address:

Phone Number:

Title:

Name:

Address:

Phone Number:

Title:

Name:

Address:

Phone Number:

Title:

Name:

Address:

Phone Number:

Title:

Name:

Address:

Phone Number:

Other Important Names and Addresses

Name:

Address:

Phone Number:

Name:

Address:

Phone Number:

Name:

Address:

Phone Number:

Name:

Address:

Phone Number:

Name:

Address:

Phone Number:

Name:

Address:

Phone Number:

Name:

Address:

Phone Number:

Name:

Address:

Phone Number:

Name:

Address:

Phone Number:

Name:

Address:

Phone Number:

Name:

Address:

Phone Number:

Name:

Address:

Phone Number:

Name:

Address:

Phone Number:

Name:

Address:

Phone Number:

APPENDIX C

Medical Records

Date
_____

Attending Medical Professional:
_____

Symptoms:
_____
_____
_____
_____
_____

Questions:
_____
_____
_____
_____
_____

Results:
_____
_____
_____
_____
_____
_____

Date

Attending Medical Professional:

Symptoms:

Questions:

Results:

Date

Attending Medical Professional:

Symptoms:

Questions:

Results:

Date

Attending Medical Professional:

Symptoms:

Questions:

Results:

Date

Attending Medical Professional:

Symptoms:

Questions:

Results: